Time and Temporality in the Ancient World

TIME AND TEMPORALITY IN THE ANCIENT WORLD

Edited by
Ralph M. Rosen

UNIVERSITY OF PENNSYLVANIA MUSEUM
OF ARCHAEOLOGY AND ANTHROPOLOGY

Copyright © 2004
by
University of Pennsylvania Museum of Archaeology and Anthropology
3260 South Street • Philadelphia, PA 19104–6324

All rights reserved.
First Edtion.

Cataloging-in-Publication Data on file
at the U.S. Library of Congress

Printed in the United States of America on acid-free paper

CONTENTS

Preface vii

ANCIENT TIME ACROSS TIME
   Ralph M. Rosen 1

1 TEMPORALITY AND THE STUDY OF PREHISTORY
   John C. Barrett 11

2 SHAPING LIFE IN THE LATE PREHISTORIC AND
  ROMANO-BRITISH PERIODS
   Chris Gosden 29

3 SCHOLARLY CONCEPTIONS AND QUANTIFICATIONS OF TIME
  IN ASSYRIA AND BABYLONIA, C. 750–250 BCE
   Eleanor Robson 45

4 CONCEPTS OF TIME IN CLASSICAL INDIA
   Ludo Rocher 91

5 CYCLICAL AND TELEOLOGICAL TIME IN THE HEBREW BIBLE
   Marc Brettler 111

6 TEMPORALITY AND THE FABRIC OF SPACE-TIME IN
  EARLY CHINESE THOUGHT
   David W. Pankenier 129

7 TOPOGRAPHIES OF TIME IN HESIOD
   Alex Purves 147

8 GREEK CHRONOGRAPHIC TRADITIONS ABOUT THE FIRST
  OLYMPIC GAMES
   Astrid Möller 169

9 PAGAN AND CHRISTIAN NOTIONS OF THE WEEK IN THE
  4TH CENTURY CE WESTERN ROMAN EMPIRE
   Michele Renee Salzman 185

Contributors 213

Index 214

PREFACE

The chapters in this volume were originally presented at a conference at the University of Pennsylvania in April 2002, "Time and Temporality in the Ancient World," which I organized in my capacity that year as Director of the Center for Ancient Studies. This turned out to be a truly interdisciplinary event, memorable not only for the number and variety of disciplines represented, but also for the sense of a coherent and common enterprise among all participants. It is a pleasure, therefore, to present here a selection of contributions from the conference, which I hope will convey to the reader something of the collaborative spirit that suffused it.

The conference was funded by the Center for Ancient Studies, with assistance from the Department of Classical Studies at Penn, and I am grateful to both for also helping to support the production of this volume. Greatest thanks, of course, go to the participants themselves at the conference. All of them contributed in important ways to what became a uncommon moment of intellectual community, and the presence even of those not represented in this volume can still be felt in these essays. Walda C. Metcalf, Director of Publications at the University of Pennsylvania Museum of Archaeology and Anthroplogy, took a deep interest in this project from the very beginning, and I thank her for her energy and intellectual acumen at every stage. I have had invaluable technical and editorial assistance from Andrew Korzeniewski, and am especially grateful to him for his ability to assimilate a diversity of scholarly styles into a coherent whole, and always without a single complaint. Finally, I thank my colleague in the Department of the History of Art, Holly Pittman, whose unwavering commitment to the interdisciplinary study of antiquity has been a source of inspiration to me since the days when she served as the first Director of the Center for Ancient Studies.

ANCIENT TIME ACROSS TIME

Ralph M. Rosen

When the Center for Ancient Studies was founded at the University of Pennsylvania in 1996, its guiding mission was to encourage scholars of pre-modern cultures to interact in fruitful ways with each other, without fear of crossing traditional disciplinary, geographical, or methodological boundaries. There will always be plenty of localized research to perform on any given culture, highly contingent upon historical or environmental circumstances, but even within this context, when we encounter the most fundamental questions of humanity, we often find ourselves craving comparative data. This is especially the case when we are confronted with phenomena that seem at odds with the sensibilities of our own era, for it is often comparanda from other fields that enable us to decide whether such phenomena are indeed idiosyncratic to a given culture or whether we simply can find no analogues for them in our own. The comparative approach is a powerful inducement for us to rethink the ways in which we reconstruct and conceptualize the individual cultures of antiquity and pre-modernity and the ways in which we study them.

It was in this comparative and collaborative spirit that the Center sponsored a conference on Time and Temporality in the Ancient World in the spring of 2002, where the chapters in this volume began their life. This event brought together a diverse group of scholars working on various aspects of time in pre-modern cultures, most of whom probably would not have anticipated how fruitful the encounter with each other was to be. The selection of essays in this collection represents well the energy and excitement that the conference generated, as speakers and audience discovered innumerable points of contact among the many fields of expertise they brought to bear on the larger theme.

As the essays in this volume indicate, there can be no doubt that the topic of time and temporality in antiquity is ideally suited to cross-cultural and interdisciplinary approaches. Although each human being presumably experiences time in a personal, idiosyncratic way, the phenomenon itself has a distinctly universal quality about it that aligns it with the other imperatives—birth, death, hunger, gender— that all humans at all times must confront. The sun rises and sets, the heart beats, the body ages, memories form and fade; humans may conceptualize or name all these processes in vastly different ways, but they could not escape them thousands of years ago, and we cannot ourselves escape them today. All cultures—ancient and modern alike— must at some point realize that the very notion of existence implies some sense of time, whether it is a static time, time that flows in one direction like a river or that moves like a continuous circle; time that implies endless futurity or an ever-growing past. Consciousness of self—arguably the most fundamental token of humanity—implies consciousness of mortality, which in turn implies consciousness of time, for it is impossible for the sentient human being to escape the constant reminders of earthly mutability, corporeal decay, and the end of life itself. Even attempts to transcend time must come to grips with the fact that our inexorable movement from birth to death is a process, and process itself implies some sort of movement through time, whether we construe it as forward, backward, or in an endless loop.

This volume also makes clear that ancient cultures approached the question of time with as much variety and ingenuity as they applied to the other monumental questions of human existence, and there is no reason to suppose that we can legitimately articulate a comprehensive, monolithic pre-modern or ancient conception of time and temporality. Yet it is remarkable how many themes recur in these essays, how often we find homologous conceptualizations of time in cultures that had no apparent contact with one another, and how enduring certain temporal structures seem to have been across broad epochal expanses. Perhaps this should not surprise us, since the rhythm of human existence itself is so relentlessly punctuated by temporal markers, whether we think of the oscillation between day and night or the lunar and solar cycles that appear inviolately stable while our bodies inevitably deteriorate. It is no wonder that so many cultures, as the following chapters amply demonstrate, find their way to metaphors of decline and renewal, cycles, circles, and lines to assist them in expressing the peculiar ways in which time is both highly abstract and almost palpably concrete. Time and again, the essays in this collection recur to such questions in various forms, despite their broad chronological and geographical range, and when read together they provide elements of a larger story about how humans construct time and conceptualize the activities of their lives in relation to a past and future.

Our collection begins with essays by two scholars of European prehistory, John Barrett and Christopher Gosden, archaeologists who ask difficult questions about what our perennially incomplete material record can legitimately tell us both about how prehistoric people conceptualized time and how we ourselves conceptualize prehistory. Barrett moves deftly between second-order questions of how archaeological procedure conceptualizes temporality—with its concern to recover moments in time or events in their relation to the processes that are often held to account for them— and how Bronze Age Europeans may have themselves conceptualized time. Barrett is concerned not so much with how such peoples self-consciously expressed and represented time (questions which are nearly unanswerable in any case, given the nature of the evidence), but rather in how their systems of land tenure and their burial practices seem to arise as a function of changing concepts of temporality and, as he puts it, "temporal reasoning."

Gosden is likewise interested in what we can infer from the archaeological record—for example, building practices, the construction of public works—about how ancient societies conceptualized time, even when we lack textual or iconographic evidence for a specific temporal self-consciousness. Focusing on a single site in England which he has excavated, "Alfred's Castle," Gosden describes how its Romano-British occupants evidently forged distinct links with an Iron Age past, already quite remote in time from them, by interpolating their forms of linear ditch-digging into ditch systems in place since the Iron Age. The Romano-British period was obviously a time of flux and transformation and, one assumes, at least some degree of anxiety, as the native inhabitants of Britain assimilated Roman practices. Gosden argues for a "wholesale re-attachment of people to things" in this period of Romanization and suggests that this process may well have stimulated an increased self-consciousness about an individual's place within a temporal continuum.

Many of the methodological and epistemological uncertainties that archaeologists such as Barrett and Gosden must contend with become less profound for cultures which happen to have left us a textual tradition. In the case of ancient Babylonia and Assyria, as Eleanor Robson amply shows, the enormous number of cuneiform clay tablets that have survived to our time affords us an often remarkably detailed view of how these cultures conceptualized time and, indeed, how they constructed their lives around very specific, institutionalized temporal schemata. Robson is particularly interested in the scholarly tradition in ancient Assyria and Babylonia which was largely responsible for formulating the systems of marking time that ultimately informed many aspects of ritual and public policy. As Robson shows, these scholarly sages, usually attached to royal houses in advisory capacities, were largely focused on the task of interpreting the will of the gods as it was manifested in terrestrial or celestial signs, such as planetary or stellar movements, and, especially, the cycles of the sun and moon. Robson's discussion reveals a fascinating moment of intellectual history where acute empirical—some might say proto-scientific—observation intersected with traditional belief systems. The result, as Robson demonstrates, was an extraordinarily elaborate calendrical system, rooted in precise mathematical and astronomical formulations, but largely in the service of the great non-scientific goals that still interest us today, namely, how to understand and, one hopes, control the forces of good and evil that pervade the world.

Ludo Rocher notes in his chapter the influence of Babylonian astronomy and mathematics on classical Indian conceptions of time, as well as the likelihood that Greek thought also informed Indian theories of cyclic time and "world ages" (known as a yuga/kalpa system). But Rocher argues that these theories may well have had indigenous origins within Indian culture itself and need not have been appropriated wholesale from other cultures. Despite interesting coincidences between the Indian concept of the kalpa (a term referring to a period of time, frequently associated with specifically divine time) and Babylonian numerology, Rocher argues that Indian notions of temporal cycles could well have developed independently of professional astronomers and philosophers, especially foreign ones, such as the Babylonian ummanu he discusses. Rocher further challenges a well-known *argumentum ex silentio*, namely that the yuga/kalpa system of cyclical time must be post-Vedic because it is not mentioned in the Vedic literature. Rocher points out that Vedic texts had, in fact, a limited audience and can hardly be taken to represent the views of contemporary Indian society as a whole. Rocher does find evidence that these texts allude to notions of cyclical time, even if they do not explicitly describe them. Ultimately, Rocher would like to locate the origins of the yuga/kalpa system in an extra-Vedic space, that is, among a broader population of nonspecialists who would have been as deeply sensitive to the cycles and temporal markers of the natural world around them as any self-styled intellectual of the day.

As this collection shows, one of the most persistent dichotomies we find across many pre-modern societies is that between cyclical and teleological time. The choices seem clear enough: one considers the inevitable progression of a human life from birth to death and concludes that time marches inexorably forward toward a telos, or goal. At the same time, this apparently linear progression of a human life span is situated within the temporal markers of nature that seem repetitive, cyclical, and fundamentally stable through time. As these essays make clear, over the millennia much ingenuity has been directed at these apparently contradictory models of time, as people variously attempted either to reconcile them, privilege one over the other, or explain them in terms that leave empiricism or human rationality behind.

Marc Brettler discusses precisely this tension between teleological (or eschatological) and cyclical, periodically recurrent time in the Hebrew Bible. Despite the fact that the Bible does not offer much in the way of second-order, philosophical discourse about time, many passages suggest a notion of cyclical time. Brettler examines the evidence of Ecclesiastes and Judges, in particular, that at least some ancient Israelites believed that events recur through time, although only God controls and can understand why things happen when and as they do. Biblical scholars, however, have often contrasted this notion with what they believe to be a distinct eschatological strand elsewhere in the Bible, especially in the books of the Prophets, which often speak of the "end of time." As earlier scholars have pointed out, such prophecies for the future usually involve a return to a past state or past conditions within Israel's history, and Brettler argues that it is inaccurate and misleading to refer to such periods as "eschatological" in the sense of a telos arrived at in a linear temporal progression. While the Bible does not explicitly address the many questions that arise when one juxtaposes a prophetic future time with an over-all scheme of cyclical time, Brettler maintains that the two notions are far less contradictory than has often been supposed.

Within the field of scholarship on ancient China, a similar debate has also emerged over whether this culture subscribed predominantly to a linear or cyclical conception of time. As David Pankenier points out, scholars in recent decades have tended to regard the conception of time in ancient China as, on the whole, basically linear and irreversible. Pankenier shows how Western scholars might indeed reach such a sweeping conclusion and in what senses it accurately characterizes certain aspects of ancient China. But he proceeds to argue that our own notions of temporality, history, and causation often impede a deeper understanding of how ancient Chinese culture (insofar as one can even speak so categorically of such a complex and diverse culture) actually conceptualized the relationship among events through time. Pankenier stresses an early Chinese idea of "connectedness" and "correspondence" among events that does not always imply causation or a traditional Western sense of ordered temporality. His close textual analysis of a work by the influential Han dynasty philosopher, Dong Zhongshu, uncovers in Dong's hexagrams from *The Book of Changes* a metaphorical conceptualization of time and history drawn from weaving, where the warp and weft of a fabric proceed in a direction simultaneously linear and recursive, but with a resulting pattern that can only be comprehended as a totality that emerges from their interrelationship. As Pankenier's essay makes clear, a variety of metaphors for time were available to the ancient Chinese, depending on one's particular perspective. Some of these were highly concrete and spatial, others more abstract and symbolic.

Alex Purves finds a similar diversity and boldness of metaphor in archaic Greece in her essay on the epic poet Hesiod. Purves principally seeks here to analyze the organization of time in Hesiod's *Theogony*, a poem that explicitly problematizes the question of divine and human temporality. Ostensibly concerned with a genealogy of the gods—the defeat of older, past generations, by a newer one that "always is" —the *Theogony* recounts the process by which the eternally present Zeus actually manipulates time by incarcerating the older gods (who represent past time) under the earth while physically ingesting the potential for a future time, namely, Zeus's offspring. Hesiod is able to conceptualize time as something that can be contained, whether it be in the vessel of Zeus's body or in a prison beneath the earth. If all this seems rather poetic and remote from the lived reality of ancient Greece, Purves astutely discusses how in his other great poem, *Works and Days*—a very different sort of effort set in the form of a didactic "farmer's almanac"—Hesiod can again use concrete spatial metaphors of containment (jars, pails, granaries) to describe time, but here in the context of agriculture and household management. While the temporal cycles of the natural world (days, seasons) recur in a predictable, seemingly endless, fashion, Hesiod's farmer, like Zeus himself in the *Theogony*, can intervene and exercise some control over the effects of time on his own life.

One area in which all ancient cultures struggled to control and organize time was in chronography, the very practical business of keeping records, dating events, marking historical intervals, and periodizing their own histories. Each of the cultures examined in this collection developed idiosyncratic methods of situating themselves relative to a past and present (and sometimes even to a future), and each had to confront the question of how to construct chronological reference points. Astrid Möller tells the fascinating story of how ancient Greek chronography came to adopt the foundation of the Olympic games as their chief chronographical reference point. The 5th century BCE sophist, Hippias of Elis, is generally credited with attempting to synchronize historical events in relation to the Olympic games, though the question of whether he actually fixed the traditional foundation date of the games to what we would call 776 BCE remains unresolved, given the insufficient state of our evidence (no parts of an actual text of Hippias's alleged treatise on the Olympic games survive). Despite a scholarly tradition that takes a rather dim of view of Hippias's actual contribution to Greek chronography, however, Möller argues for the foundational importance of his treatise and charts the subsequent efforts of Hellenistic and late antique scholars to build upon his initial collection of Olympic victors.

Our volume concludes with an essay by Michele Renee Salzman in which she examines one ancient system of conceptualizing time—the notion of a week—that still persists, in variant forms, throughout much of the world today. We tend to take for granted the notion of the seven-day "week," along with our focus on Sunday as a marked day of rest, as a fundamental mechanism of marking time within a year. But as Salzman shows, the modern week evolved from a complex interaction of pagan and Christian cultural practices during the 4th century CE. Salzman focuses in particular on the early history of Sunday (the dies Solis or "Day of the Sun") as a day of rest or worship—institutionalized as law by Constantine in 321—and shows that it actually took quite a long time for the idea to catch on, largely, it seems, because it was an innovation without clear precedent in pagan culture.

We find in this collection, then, a diversity of approaches to the topic of time in antiquity—some contributors working primarily with material and textual culture, some focusing on distinctions between sacred and secular time, some on metaphors from the mythic imaginary, and others examining the various ways in which ancient societies harnessed time for utilitarian or chronographical ends. Juxtaposing these cultures will yield remarkable intersections and continuities, as well as discontinuities, in the ways in which each engages with time and temporality. It is to be hoped that readers who come to this collection from a specific discipline of their own will be able to see how often the insights of one essay have implications for another and how, in turn, this interdisciplinary enterprise will enrich the study of time in even the most historically contingent contexts.

1

TEMPORALITY AND THE STUDY OF PREHISTORY

John C. Barrett

Without writing, and thus without calendars, the periods of prehistory seem unlikely to contribute much to our enquiry into ancient concepts of time. We could argue that while the archives of prehistory lack a written testimony they nevertheless cover the greater part of human history and thus bear witness to considerable changes in the scale, organization, and material expression of the human condition. It might follow that prehistory should have something to offer that is original and interesting. Even so, the claim that what we lose in detail we gain in scale seems poor recompense for the apparent lack of the intimate understanding of human history that becomes possible once written and oral testimonies are available. This chapter will make the case for a prehistory of temporality and set out the basis upon which such a prehistory might operate.

I will begin by assessing the claim that prehistorians work best, and should therefore restrict themselves almost exclusively to, broad-scale analysis with its long-term perspective on human history. I will then illustrate the issues covered by considering a particular transformation that occurred in the first half of the 2nd millennium BCE in northern Europe, a period toward the middle of the Bronze Age that witnessed various changes in agricultural organization, including the more intensive use of land, increasing population, and the general emergence of longer-lived nucleated settlements.

The Problematic Relationships between Event, Process, and Structural History in Archaeology

Prehistory seems best understood at the larger scale when tracing long-term changes in the material organization of human activity. However, at such a scale we see the patterns of the past without necessarily understanding the mechanisms that carried these particular histories forward. The question of how these patterns were generated cannot be answered by limiting our analysis to long-term trajectories; instead it requires some engagement with the detailed and fine-grained nature of human life. The implication is that human history—using the term in its broadest sense, as concerning the human past, not restricting its use to the presence of written records—is not built at a single temporal scale. Consequently we need to establish a clearer understanding of the ways different temporal scales of historical process operate in relation one to the other. Any assertion that prehistory must, by necessity, give predominance to one scale (long-term trajectories of change) at the expense of another (short-term and local events) is therefore erroneous. It is surprising that archaeology has not discussed these issues more fully. As Bailey (1981) noted: "As a discipline which expends a large part of its resources on dating and chronology, archaeology has made remarkably little contribution to the elaboration of time concepts, perhaps all the more surprising in a discipline concerned with time spans far beyond what is customary in the studies of the anthropologist or the historian" (102).

The issue demanding clarification concerns the distinction usually drawn between *event* and *process*. As commonly used, events are treated as singular and bracketed in time, while processes are treated in terms of their continuity through time. Processes may also be characterized in more general terms; they are processes of a certain type. We can make the distinction between event and process because we are content to use time as the axis on which events are mapped and through which processes flow; time acts as our independent axis of measurement and definition. As we shall see, the event/process distinction underpins the logic of current archaeological practice and it hinders interpretation.

The relationship between the moment of time (event) and its continuity (process) has been widely addressed. Within the historical disciplines the simplest models evoke the imagery of levels of historical time, metaphorically juxtaposing a surface of transient events upon mechanisms operating over the long term. The argument may lead us to the unremarkable conclusion that forces cause events, but the implications are rather more important. The forces of history, from this perspective, appear to be endowed with continuity over the long term and explain from whence events arise as consequences. The long term therefore appears to determine and explain the general direction of history, where the occurrences of specific events map the "conjunctures" of these forces and the operation of localized constraints. The imagery is certainly effective. Events appear to be thrown up as the passing and material manifestations of underlying forces in the way that the catastrophe of a particular earthquake is the product of plate tectonics impacting upon particular surface conditions.

An understanding of those generative mechanisms would therefore seem to necessitate that we get beyond the immediacy of the event because its historical significance is contingent upon the continuity of forces operating on a much larger scale. Let us refer to these generative mechanisms or forces as the structuring of history where the term "structure" is used as a verb. This usage has an important implication: to structure something must involve the event of actually doing the structuring. The distinction between process as cause and event as consequence is therefore less clear cut than it seems at first. Processes must be generated through the workings of events.

Prehistorians have obviously found appeals for the writing of "structural" histories enticing because they seem to describe what they see themselves as doing. The problem is that prehistorians, and indeed archaeologists in general, simply equate long-term sequences of material conditions (things that can be traced over a long period of time) with the structuring of history. This fails to take account of the moments in which the structuring of history is necessarily realized.

The confusion may arise in the way the word "process" finds two different usages in archaeology. One is as the description of the unfolding of events over a long time span, such as the "process of agricultural intensification" that may be mapped, for example, by a sequence of increasingly large grain stores associated with crop remains of increasing purity. The other is as a generative process that attempts to explain the trajectory of, for example, agricultural intensification. The latter might appear to be driven by various relationships among a growing population, innovations in technology, and developing land management. It is in the second and active sense that process is misleadingly equated with the structuring of history. Thus, archaeologists can refer to the process of the adoption of agriculture both as if they were describing the sequence of material conditions that takes us from hunter-gatherers to farmers and as if they were explaining why the change occurs. However, all that has been achieved is a simple reduction where sequences of material are presented as if they were a direct manifestation of the real dynamic of history, in the way that a long-term sequence of residues deriving from changing agricultural activities is falsely equated with the structural history of agricultural change itself.

In archaeology, events are manifest empirically in the material record; we observe the result of events in the residues from their execution. What exactly structured these histories, what brought such events into play in certain ways, seems less clearly attested if not actually entirely mysterious. It is as if we witness the passing of history as a trajectory without grasping what had driven that trajectory forward.

The alternative is perhaps to treat archaeological events and processes as different perceptions of the same historical mechanism, an alternative view that becomes possible if we do two things. First, we abandon the treatment of time as an absolute and independent medium along which our various histories have moved. Time is not a condition that is independent of the material conditions of history; rather it is constituted in those conditions. Second, we treat the *structuring* of history as the active condition within which temporalities are formed and which is manifested as archaeological events and processes. Structuring is therefore the event in which past conditions may be mobilised by future intentions.

This may all sound very abstract, but the reality of the issue is best grasped by reference to the problems archaeology faces in its various attempts to move both from the description of what happened and to offer an interpretation of human history. These fundamental problems result from the distinction archaeology currently attempts to maintain between event and process. It will therefore be necessary to understand why such a distinction seems necessary and therefore un-contentious in current archaeological practice before proceeding toward an attempt to transcend these limitations.

The Archaeological Procedure

Archaeology uses the material consequences of formation events as its empirical evidence. From this perspective, long sequences of material appear to describe a historical trajectory of events. Archaeology is proficient at establishing the nature of those events that are implicated in the creation of some portion of the material record. The interpretive problem is to explain the history of events. Such explanations are usually couched in terms of process, where processes appear to act as a kind of motor or agency for history and where generative processes are often taken to be represented by multiple and sequential events. Processes, in other words, appear to make things happen.

It would seem that archaeological evidence (the material residue) now has two jobs to do—first, to provide evidence of the nature and development of historical conditions (a sequence); second, to provide evidence that enables us to identify the processes that brought those historical conditions into being. It is unlikely that the evidence can do both, but the deeper problem is that we are using process to describe a trajectory of consequences and to explain that trajectory causally. However, given that causes cannot be their own consequences it is hardly surprising that the explanations offered appear less than substantial. The failure signals the gap in reasoning that separates the event, as the problem to be explained, from the process that supposedly does the explaining.

The premise underpinning all archaeological analysis is that material residues derived from the human past not only survive but are interpretable from the viewpoint of our contemporary world. Archaeological procedures aim to establish the form and the historical significance of the surviving record. Form concerns physical characterisation, and we can establish a great deal about the physical processes contributing to the form of the record. The historical significance of the record on the other hand concerns the reasons for the regularities of past events and thus the reasons for the regularities of human behavior.

Analysis must therefore move beyond the description of what happened in the past to explain why things happened the way they did. The initial recording procedures of field archaeology privilege the event as that which needs explaining. They isolate individual stratigraphic contexts and by cataloging the relationships of one context to another; they move from the record of stratigraphic events to a sequence of stratigraphy that records a series of formation events. Processes initially identified in terms of cumulative events set us on the path toward isolating generative processes of explanation. Economic processes generate cumulative events relating to material production, whereas cumulative events relating to mortuary rituals may result from processes of social display. Thus, the prehistorian synthesizes what might appear to be a partial record of events into a larger pattern of processes (a pattern of things that happened). This pattern, in turn, automatically implies the generative process that will be used to explain that pattern.

Identifying process as mere repetition is not explanation. But if explanation lies in understanding the reasons for the repetition and the reasons for the direction of the cumulative events resulting from that repetition, then we must identify why specific trajectories of events took place through time. This in turn requires the identification of an agency to drive a specific trajectory. We may see now the way patterns of material traced over large areas, or sequences of material traced over long periods of time, offer the image of large-scale and long-term processes whose explanation then appears to require the identification of a generative process, and thus an agency, that operated on a similar scale. Thus, we arrive at the prehistorian's interest in explanations in terms of long-term so-called structural histories where events are products of those histories. However, the mistake throughout is to equate process (as simply a pattern of change) with structural histories.

It would be difficult to overestimate the importance of these issues in light of the significant confusions and false expectations they have generated. If a sequence of events demarcates the trajectory of a process, then not only does that process obviously have a direction, but any explanation for the sequence is expected to offer a causal explanation for why that direction occurred. The trap is sprung when we imbue the generative process with an intentional logic that operated at the same scale as the pattern being explained and which is further described entirely by the outcome of the chain of events. The generative process occurs, in other words, in order to do what it achieves. Functional explanations are teleological in this way, where the explanation for the process is that it existed to achieve the endpoint to which it ultimately arrives.

Let us use a single example to illustrate the point. The Bronze Age palaces on Crete arose through a sequence of building events that are interpretable in terms of the events of mechanical formation (working the materials) and the events of social convention (architectural style and decoration). However, the historical issues raised by these buildings are more complex. Scholars have sought to understand the organization of mechanisms and conventions, and they address the historical contexts within which such buildings operated at their various stages of completion. The mechanisms and conventions that governed the construction of the palaces are usually assumed to be dictated by the function of the completed buildings. Consequently, arguments concerning the role of the palaces in economic or ceremonial activities, along with ideas that their final development saw them operating as administrative centers governing regional economies, always mean that 'explanations' seek out reasons for why such facilities may have been necessary in the first place. It is these reasons (or needs) that appear to drive the process and ultimately determine the agency of the human community that actually built these structures. The extent to which that agency shared this purpose in its own motivations or foresaw their implications is questionable, as is the extent to which human projects always fulfill their purpose and never generate unintended consequences. More to the point however, the function of the palace could not exist without the palace to facilitate it, requiring as it did the material conditions of its own operation. To propose otherwise results in an infinite regress.

The common assumption, for example, that the palaces of the Middle Bronze Age were constructed to facilitate the operation of an elite and that this necessarily explains the building program, would mean that such an elite must have preexisted these palaces. Operating presumably in some primitive form that needed the palace to be built to achieve its full development, this proto-elite must have been housed in pre-palace structures in the Early Bronze Age. Needless to say, the search for such structures has become a research priority. However, these Early Bronze Age pre-palaces were presumably constructed to facilitate the needs of an even earlier proto-elite form whose existence we might find attested in the Neolithic. Continuing this way we might conclude that the Paleolithic of southern Greece must have imprinted within it the predestined need for the Bronze Age palaces.

Generative processes that explain a history of events always appear to have a general logic. We speak, for example, of explaining the origins of the Neolithic, where the explanation is singular and to which a multitude of events conform. That we have been far less successful in identifying that process might have given the hint that all was not well in the entire enterprise. Long-term and general changes in human conditions obviously occur, there was a Neolithic, but does a structural history of these changes necessitate our reliance upon these general and nonspecific processes to act as the language for its expression? Structure and process are not the same. What then are structures and how do they work? More often than not we refer to structures as constraining. Constraints may include the unequal and restricted accumulation of property, restricted access to forms of traditional authority, or the restricted control of technology. All certainly occur, but all are necessarily made to work at various moments in their various ways to constrain the life chances of some and benefit others. This "making to work" certainly does not result from the vitality of material conditions; rather it is a significance necessarily created, resisted, or re-negotiated in the context of various discursive practices. Such practices demarcate the events enabled within these structural conditions and from whence their effects are realized implicitly or explicitly in the specific experiences of people's lives. It is in these moments (these events) that the character and pervasiveness of structural conditions gain their reality and the human commitment to their continuity is thus tested.* Structures link event and process and allow us to

---

* I take the post-modern "incredulity toward metanarratives" referred to by Lyotard (1984) not as a move that refuses to accept the existence of the structural conditions of history but as one that rejects the possibility that such structures both exist independently of practice and are wholly determinate of historical reality.

investigate the extent to which events actually bring processes into being. Events are the moments of making things happen, the movement from a past state of affairs toward a future condition. Events involve various forms of agency that expend energy and do work. Making an object may contribute to carrying forward the economic process, but the process does not determine the event. If this is accepted then the historical problem is to understand how events are structured to follow a particular trajectory (where that trajectory may be described as a particular type of process).

The Structural Conditions of Agency

The terms *structure* and *agency* are used widely enough and in such divergent ways that any brief employment here risks confusion. However, these terms provide the means to avoid the pitfalls so far identified—my argument has been that the concept of *process* in archaeology has little if any explanatory value. Process is simply the map of patterns of continuity and changes in events through time. Attempts to extend the concept of process to incorporate generative procedures result in a reification where the appearance of material change becomes an expression of the real force of historical change. The failure of this reasoning is witnessed simply by the fact that we still have so little idea about the processes behind the origins of agriculture, chiefdoms, or the state. These may be big questions, but the big answers have been slow in coming. In their place we are presented with tautologies which simply state that for such systems to emerge, the conditions by which they are defined have to exist. Events and processes are ways of charting the conditions of human existence through time and nothing more; they are descriptive.

Agency on the other hand makes things happen, intervening in the world by converting energy and doing work, and it makes things happen out of the conditions of the moment. Human beings are one type of agency that is particular in the ways that it is conscious, the ways it seeks to place itself in the world, and the ways it claims the understanding of others. Structures are the possibilities that exist for that agency to place itself in history. Structures are realized when agency finds ways of linking the past to the future and in the ways agency may ultimately link the local and particular conditions of life to the larger and largely unimagined movements of history. The strategies human agents use to carry the regularities of life forward in the contexts of other cumulative changes occurring in the wider environment can result in significant and long-term material and institutional transformations. Such transformations are rarely if ever planned. Indeed, when attempts have been made to plan such transformations the results more often than not have been disastrous for those communities who are the object of such planning. Life may be directed toward distant goals, but these are not the same as the necessarily unknowable outcomes, unknowable simply because the material terms in which they will be defined have yet to exist.

The structural conditions of possibility are what enable human agency to contribute to the making of history. It is only a contribution; other agencies are also at work to change and transform the material conditions of life, but the human contribution most concerns us. The temporal definition of human agency is not a question of the moment when it acts (the event). The prehistorian does not investigate human agency by identifying the acts of an individual. Nor is the temporal definition a matter of fixing its position in a sequence of events (process), as if that sequence were in some way determined by its own logic and the actions of human agency were therefore similarly determined. Rather, temporal definition comes with an understanding of how it was possible for agents to establish a place for themselves in their own histories and what the larger consequences of those strategies may have been.

Bronze Age Transformations

Despite the doubts shared toward 19th century schemes of technological evolution, it is still common to find prehistorians identifying the Bronze Age with a particular stage in human social development. Earle (2002), for example, argues that with the Bronze Age we witness the transformation of subsistence economies and the beginning of a "political economy." The distinction he draws is between economies in which households maintained themselves in relative autonomy and economies whereby surpluses were "mobilized and allocated to support political activities, lifestyles, and operations of social institutions and their leaders." He continues: "By practical control, political economies are built on subsistence economies and together organize all production, distribution, and consumption. The three factors of production are land, labour, and capital" (Earle 2002:9).

The distinction between subsistence and political economies, along with the notion that the latter evolves from the former, and with the general claim of the applicability of this sequence on a world scale, presents a challenge to explain the process with reference to some general logic. It is certainly true that the archaeological evidence associated with Bronze Age societies does indicate that they were characterized by large-scale networks of exchange, complex craft production, increasing levels of agricultural production, the existence of rich burial assemblages, and a considerable mobilization of labor and material investment in the maintenance of monumental centers. These are economies of scale. We may also, if we wish, arrange these economies in a sequence between the more localized production and exchange that is characteristic of social orders based upon kinship and the larger-scale political organizations that operated beyond the obligations of kinship and which are characterized by the politics of the state. We may further recognize that such a general order of scale is matched by particular trajectories of development where the sequence is played out historically.

The historical problem of Bronze Age economies (if we allow ourselves to follow Earle's terminology) does not come down to isolating a single process or trajectory of development by which to explain their apparent regularities. Rather it is to trace the structural conditions of possibility, that is the diversity of conditions out of which new and at times similar forms of order arose at different times, in different places, and from diverse conditions. Thus, we may accept that the Bronze Age does represent a single condition on a world scale and concerns the emergence of a particular structure of organization without necessarily seeking a single historical explanation. Such a program of analysis is empirical inasmuch as it concerns itself with the operation of particular historical conditions and their possible consequences.

This has significant implications for archaeological practice. Normative procedures seek generalizations about the form of the evidence as representative of social or economic conditions. This allows for a simplification and characterization of diverse and complex sets of data. Indeed this is how we have already treated the evidence for the Bronze Age. However, the material must do a lot more than this. For it to work as the basis of historical understanding it must not be reduced from the representations of particular events to a characterization of a type of process. Instead, the evidence must address the conditions of possibility for human agency.

Among the general characteristics of Bronze Age economies identified by Earle is the emergence of a land tenure that permitted direct control over production, either by the community or some portion of the community, along with the development of technologies of more intensive agricultural production, and the inheritance of rights of access from one generation to the next. This general condition contributes to the characterization of Bronze Age economies, and our historical understanding of that condition must concern the particular conditions of possibility from whence it arose. There is no one answer and no single line of causality. However, given that tenure concerns a form of temporal reasoning in that it binds people and resources together over time, then we might expect that changes in tenure can only have arisen in part through changes in that temporal reasoning.

Our investigation is now concerned with the conditions under which changing concepts of temporality may have arisen, and the evidence we draw upon must therefore be relevant to this issue. I would stress that this is not the same as treating the material evidence as the representation of concepts of temporality, in the way a historian may treat a text as representing a calendrical system. We are concerned with the conditions of making the world rather than expressing it. This allows us a certain degree of flexibility in the investigation of temporality, for prehistorians need not despair that they have no representations of the idea but rather explore, optimistically, the diversity of material locations in which the concept may have been formulated. To this end, we shall to consider very briefly the changing treatment of the dead between the Neolithic and Bronze Age in one part of Britain.

Megalithic tombs are characteristic of many parts of the western European Neolithic. Variable in design and covering a very broad chronological range in their histories of construction and use, these monuments usually contain the mixed and partial skeletal remains of a number of individuals. The architecture often involves some form of access between the outside world and the inner chambers, and the mixed and often partial representation of much of the surviving skeletal material evokes ideas of repeated use and cumulative deposition. Indeed the elaboration of these monuments through the deposition of human remains, artifacts, and, at times almost continual, structural modification, would imply they became repositories of labor, history, and emotional commitment for the communities within which they operated.

The megalithic tomb of West Kennet, on the chalk uplands of southern Britain, is among those that appear a typical example of such Neolithic monuments. For our purposes this role in representing the processes of mortuary rites in the period takes us no further analytically. Instead we shall treat West Kennet as a specific location at which a change in the reckoning of time became possible. At one stage in its history five stone built chambers were situated at the end of a long mound, and these contained the disarticulated skeletal remains of a number of individuals. These remains were partial, and some had been stacked in a relatively orderly manner at the back of the chambers. The chambers themselves opened onto a gallery entered through the center of a curving façade. Toward the end of the 3rd millennium BCE the chambers were infilled using a mixture of chalk rubble, soil, and artifact debris. The infilling was accompanied by a redesign of the façade with the erection of a line of massive stones across and blocking the earlier approach to the entrance. The chambers and old entrance were now effectively sealed.

Most accounts refer to these acts as if they were "final," where the blocking of the chambers marked the abandonment of the tomb. It is an interesting argument, displaying all the logic of regarding the monument as intended to fulfill a single function, and that once that function was no longer possible the monument had simply lost its purpose. The alternative is to recognize that the redesigning was actually facilitating the redesigning of the acts and rites of access and co-presence that were established between the living community and the dead. This redesigning was not the abandonment or forgetting of the monument and its contents; rather it was the displacement of those contents and thus a displacement of the dead. Physically separated and now also inaccessible the dead remained but as if in another place out of reach of the contemporary world.

When this redesign of access was occurring, a new tradition of mortuary activity was also emerging in the region. Classically referred to as a single grave tradition, the burials involved dug graves with the deposition of bodies, often flexed and accompanied by a small set of artifacts arranged around the corpse (see Barrett 1994). Traditionally this material has been taken to herald a process of social change where the burial associations are assumed to reflect new levels of status among an emergent social elite. What is overlooked is that these graves are normally reopened and are used for a short sequence of inhumations, sometimes with the additions of cremations. Located as single and distinctive points in the landscape, the graves therefore mapped unique sequences of relationships between those included in the graves and relationships of close affinity or of difference, depending upon their location, among those assigned to neighboring or more distant plots.

None of this material belongs to the Middle Bronze Age, that period in which we begin to see the clearest evidence for more intensive agricultural systems and longer-lived settlements, all of which may represent the changes in land tenure suggested by Earle. None of this material seems to relate directly to agricultural practice either. My argument is that these changes in the treatment of the dead, often analyzed as a process of changing burial rites and indicative of the emergence of social hierarchies, may have had an even more profound historical implication. These mechanisms, the displacement of the dead community and the sequential linking of funerary rites to a lineage of earlier activities, may all have been among the local and specific strategies by which it was possible to formulate changes in the conceptions of temporality. These were not so much intellectual advances as the practical realization that the past, separated from the present, was also linked to it by the lineal flow of time. Along this trajectory some mediation between the past and present was possible, perhaps in funerary rites, but also perhaps in terms of the transference of rites across generations which may in turn have allowed clearer lines of tenurial rights to have been demarcated. If the Middle Bronze Age required these changes to have been put in place, then it arose not as the planned but as the unintended consequences of the temporal practices in the centuries that preceded it.*

---

*The ideas expressed in this chapter have developed as part of a longer working program I have undertaken with Stephanie Koerner, and I am grateful to her for her continual force of argument and direction, without necessarily implicating her in what appears here. Finally I must thank Cat Howarth for assisting in the final stages of writing what had become a far more complex chapter than I had originally intended.

References

Bailey, Geoff. "Concepts, Time-scales, and Explanations in Economic Prehistory." In Alison Sheridan and Geoff Bailey, eds., *Economic Archaeology: Towards an Integration of Ecological and Social Approaches*. Oxford: BAR International Ser. 96, 1981, 97-117.

Barrett, John C. *Fragments from Antiquity: An archaeology of social life in Britain, 2900–1200 BC*. Oxford: Blackwell, 1994.

Childe, V. Gordon. "The Bronze Age." *Past and Present* 12 (1957):2–15.

Earle, Timothy K. *Bronze Age Economies: The Beginnings of Political Economies*. Oxford: Westview Press, 2002.

Lyotard, Jean François. *The Postmodern Condition: A Report on Knowledge*. Manchester: Manchester University Press, 1984.

● ● 2 ● ●

SHAPING LIFE IN THE LATE PREHISTORIC AND ROMANO-BRITISH PERIODS

Chris Gosden

Time in contemporary Western thought is generally seen as a quantity, its measurable properties and its scarcity seemingly its most salient characteristics. To see time as a quantity is a mistake, as we shall see, and although it can be seen as linear and as divided into discrete units, this is just one set of conventions for making time useful in a world where time is intimately linked to money. For the (pre)historian measured time is also vital, but as a tool and ordering device, not as an essential insight into the human relationship with time. Time is shaped by the qualities of human experiences and actions in the world. In turn, actions and experiences differ from one culture to another so there are many, culturally based forms of time, not just one. We do not pass through time; time passes through us. We shall first consider the qualities of human involvement with the world, before examining a period at the end of prehistory in Britain when new relationships with the world came into being.

The Russian novelist Dostoyevsky was once condemned to death by firing squad. Standing in a line of people being shot one by one, he worked out how many minutes of life he had left and apportioned his remaining time (using a nearby church clock) into several minutes thinking about the wonder of the world, several minutes thinking about his own life, and the last few minutes getting ready for death. One of his thoughts in the later minutes was if he survived that he would try to live his life at a similar level of intensity. He was reprieved (a typical Tsarist trick which sent some people mad with relief) and of course did not live the whole of his life with similar intensity. Dostoyevsky's work was a significant inspiration for the existentialist movements of the 20th century, which focused on the nature of human relationships with the world, especially alienation. His, and their, point was that time contracts and dilates so that not all minutes are equal in experience even though, by definition, each 60 seconds is the same when measured by a clock.

Dostoyevsky's experience of time was a general human experience of time ebbing and flowing pushed to a cruel extreme. If all human life consists of periods of different length and impact of experience, of hours that fly by unnoticed or minutes that creep, we need to ask why these differences occur. Considering time more broadly we become aware that many cultures have different means of thinking and speaking about time: people who face the past with their backs to the future; those who see time as moving in cycles rather than in a linear fashion; the idea that ancestors and their actions are both infinitely removed in time, but also present in the contemporary world.

In a lucid and clear exposition of different conceptions of time Gell (1992) concludes that although people represent time very differently around the world, there is in fact only one time, which is that of the Western physicist or time-and-motion expert, linear and measurable. Gell's view privileges representations and ways of talking about time, and this is valuable.

Cartographers have engaged in much useful study into the history of map making, looking at the changing conventions used to depict space. A similar exercise is needed charting the history of temporality—the changing conventions used to represent time. However, there is always a complex relationship between representation and the manner in which temporality derives from the routines of life. Conventions of representation are not so much right or wrong, but rather more or less useful, and this is as true for the analyst as it is when we are engaged in everyday life. Calendars and radiocarbon years are vital devices for orienting ourselves, but they do not give us vital clues as to the nature of times past and there is always the danger that we will mistake the convention for the shape of social time. Time is not one thing. It is many, and its multiplicity derives from deep variations in human actions, thought, and feeling.

Life concerns attaching values to experience through making valuations of people and objects and the links between the two. Recent work on the emotions has striven to break the division between thought and emotion by showing that emotions are means of directing attention toward people and things in ways deriving from human intention (Nussbaum 2002; Reddy 2001). In such views, perception is not a passive act. It is both interested and directed; it is also linked to action. Love, hate, disgust, or compassion are means of perceiving and conceiving of the world, of people and things. Nussbaum argues that each of us learns in early childhood various discriminations attaching to things—comforting, disturbing or alienating—so each of us carries these discriminations through life. Individually our lives are complex in a temporal sense as patterns of valuation and emotion created in early childhood are carried through in the rest of our life, not mechanically enacted in all situations, but providing the basis for intelligent action within a cultural framework.

Elsewhere I have argued that our relationship with the object world through our senses can be best understood in terms of aesthetics, the sets of discriminations of taste that we apply to the sensory qualities of objects and people (Gosden 2000). Aesthetics and emotions are closely linked. The discriminations of taste we make about the qualities of objects—their brilliance, dullness, or intransigence when worked—evoke emotional responses in us which give our evaluations force and social direction. Values derive from a dynamic interaction between people and the sensory properties of objects, where people are culturally sensitized from early childhood onwards to various properties and are much less aware of others.

Perception is part and parcel of working in and on the world, and such work always has a temporal dimension. Human actions have complex sequences through the deployment of skills and abilities. Working stone into a useable implement requires a sequence of actions—the so-called *chaîne opératoire*—to reduce a large piece of stone to a smaller culturally defined tool. This sequence derives from the blows administered by the human hand, but also the flakeability of the stone and the dynamic interaction between the two. The resulting tool may be pleasing by virtue of a certain functionality, color and sheen, as well as an embodiment of human skill and care.

Skill and care are temporally structured. As Ingold (1993) has pointed out, working a landscape involves many different streams of action and involvement, with different forms of temporality linking, intertwining, or clashing (see also Gosden 1994). Climate, altitude, and latitude all influence the seasons and other forms of change within the landscape, so human skills and the inherent periodicity of the landscape grow up together in complex mutual influence.

Recent work on kinship (Carsten 2000) has shown that the patterns of relationship that are emphasized or ignored are due to patterns of action and co-habitation. Close kin are likely to be those with whom one lives and works, so the general rhythms and sequences of life feed through into patterns of human relatedness, which thus also has a temporal structure both within and across generations.

In many other areas of life, timing is all. Bourdieu (1990) pointed out that time had been ignored in studies of gift exchange which had focused most on what was given and to whom. When things are given is also vital: to return a gift too soon looks like a refusal of the relationship; to act too late makes the relationship seem unimportant. Judging the occasion and timing of a return gift is at least as important to the style and impact of the transaction as deciding what to give. Rivalries and attachments have their own forms of timing. There are, of course, long-term forms of temporality. Old sites in a landscape may be known through continuous memory of them held in oral or written form. Their origins may be lost in the mists of time, but invented anew through the creation of myth and legend. Or they may be ignored altogether as irrelevant to the workings of the contemporary world. Claims to land or legitimacy are often made through links to earlier generations and the marks they have left on the landscape. The Normans in Britain pursued the opposite strategy, constructing large, stone churches on the sites of smaller wooden Anglo-Saxon ones or positioning their castles for maximum social, as well as strategic, effect.

Time has a stratigraphic element to it, ranging from deep time embedded within the long-term use of the landscape and the marks that previous generations have left on the landscape to the individual stone-knapper sitting down for half an hour to make a flint blade. Each of these forms of temporality is calibrated against the average life span of the individual working out his or her social projects and the average life history of groups. Each social formation has its own forms of temporality compounded of a range of times from the everyday to the longest reach of history and myth. Different forms of temporality may interact; daily life is partly linked to the need to provision a longer term cycle of social exchanges and forms of ritual, so different forms of time may flow well together or clash discordantly. In all cases, time is not a neutral dimension of social life but one that takes its values from a broader set of social values and is a quality (or series of qualities) as much as a quantity.

As an example of how these rather abstract points can be applied in practice, we may briefly examine one archaeological site in southern Britain, occupied between the Iron Age and Romano-

British periods. The coming of the Romans has often been seen as the imposition of foreign values on native British culture, more particularly as the imposition of a Cartesian culture of rectangular buildings, well-laid-out streets and roads, mass-produced material culture, and a more orderly sense of time on a native consciousness less rationalized and regularized. This view is too simple, as there are complex continuities as well as changes across the Iron Age-Romano-British temporal boundary that divides prehistory from history.

"Romanization" is a contested term, but an emerging consensus is that all members of the Roman Empire participated in the construction of Roman culture, rather than having it imposed upon them. The argument is best stated by Woolf (1998) in *Becoming Roman in Gaul*, the title of the book reflecting the belief that Roman identity was a state of becoming rather than being. "Gauls were not 'assimilated' to a pre-existing social order, but participated in the creation of a new one" (Woolf 1997: 347).

Roman culture was an entity created anew in different parts of the empire at different times, through the actions of all groups, and it was not just native peoples who were being Romanized through the expansion of empire, but also the Romans themselves. If the Romanization of Britain concerned the use that was made of the new cultural resources offered by the empire we should look at the combination of existing social logics and the shape given them through participation in the empire. Time being a vital element of the social process as a whole provides us with a diagnostic of social change, so the creation of time through shaping the landscape can lead to an understanding of the novel qualities given to time after the Roman invasion of 43 CE.

Landscapes are created through repeated human actions, and the landscapes of prehistoric Britain were replete with signs of human action. Ditches and pits were dug, banks and ramparts constructed since the Neolithic period. By the period we are examining, which encompasses the late Bronze Age to the Romano-British period (the late Bronze Age lasts between roughly 1100 to 750 BCE, followed by the Iron Age which ends with the Roman invasion in 43 CE), digging and mounding were ancient traditions but were starting to be deployed in new ways. Large ditch systems, so-called linear ditches, were constructed in many areas of Britain to divide territories for reasons that we do not clearly understand. The tradition of constructing and maintaining linears lasted some thousand years until the Romano-British period. Ditches such as these, the longest of which stretch some 13 km, had not only to be dug, but also cleared regularly as water and frost eroded their sides. These features of the landscape may have names attached to them, perhaps of ancestral significance, and would have been part of the temporal round of maintaining the landscape.

Beginning in the late Bronze Age hilltops came to be enclosed, initially by relatively small ditches and banks, some of which were later enlarged in the Iron Age to become what we know as hillforts, with relatively massive ramparts and ditches which often underwent alteration. Originally seen primarily as defensive sites, as the name hillfort implies, these are now more generally viewed as sites which make a statement in the landscape to help assert social claims and to support power. I would also add that the effort of constructing these sites, the regular forms of maintenance, and work on the sites were as important as their final forms. In some sites, such as the famous Maiden Castle, there seems to have been regular small alterations to the ramparts, due to the dumping of soil in small amounts and it seems that the activity of construction may have been as important as the end result (Sharples 1991). The sites of late prehistoric southern Britain are often impressive features in themselves, which look to us to be relatively static and enduring. This should not blind us to the fact that it was actions of construction and reconstruction that may have been as important as their final form, the sites requiring regular and repeated work, all part of the temporality of the landscape.

The transition from the prehistoric to the Romano-British landscape is often seen as due to the imposition of new forms and changes in spatial sensibility. Roads, forts, and new towns created a landscape of control, which emphasized military control in the early days and the growth of trade and a healthy market as the province of Britannia developed. It is often felt that people moved out of a prehistoric world of circles or irregular lines into a more Cartesian world of squares, rectangles, and straight lines in the Romano-British period. As we shall see, this is only a partial truth. In order to address these questions, albeit in microcosm, I shall look at one particular site I have excavated together with Gary Lock, that of Alfred's Castle situated on the Berkshire Downs, part of the chalk downland that stretches across much of southern England.

Alfred's Castle, excavated over three seasons between 1998 and 2000, is a small earthwork enclosure of approximately hexagonal shape with an interior area of 1.2 ha (Figure 2.1). Surrounding the enclosure is a series of linear ditches mapped from aerial photographic evidence which form an integrated system that utilizes the contours of the local topography and is quite different from the field systems which start just to the east of the site and stretch across the Downs to the east. Integrated into the linear system is a larger enclosure that joins the northern side of the smaller hillfort enclosure.

Central to an understanding of Alfred's Castle is sequence and the way that manipulating links to the past as a form of social value appears to have influenced the development of the site. This was elucidated through the excavation of 21 trenches in all, located both within the small enclosure and around it (Figure 2.1). The earliest extant features on the site are a pair of late Bronze Age ditches, one to the west of the large and small enclosures (ditch I) and one to the southern and eastern side of the small enclosure (ditch II).

Ditch I has been visible on aerial photographs for many years and trenches 8 and 10 were positioned to explore it. Ditch 1 was a large flat-bottomed linear ditch approximately 2 m deep with fills containing pottery of probable late Bronze Age date. Ditch I represents a late Bronze Age linear as known from elsewhere on the Berkshire Downs. Trench 21 revealed that ditch I was cut by the

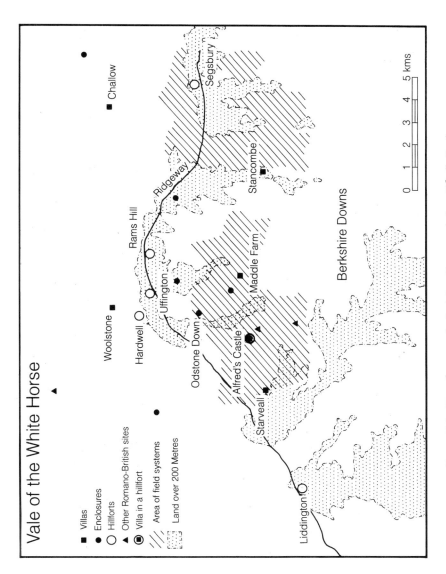

Figure 2.1 Map of sites on the Berkshire Downs including Alfred's Castle.

enclosure ditch of Alfred's Castle, ditch V, and that its end had been packed with chalk where it was cut, presumably to give the appearance of unbroken chalk along the side of the enclosure ditch.

Ditch II ran across the southern side of the site and was investigated through the trenches in area C, it was relatively shallow, but of the same flat-bottomed profile as ditch I. A terminus to the ditch was discovered at its eastern end, where it reduced its width by half, from 2 m to 1 m, and then ended. At its western end ditch II was cut through by the enclosure ditch, ditch V, which made use of the line of the earlier ditch but was much more massive than it. The linear was again packed with clean chalk where the enclosure ditch cut it, again presumably to give an appearance of an unbroken line of chalk along the side of the enclosure ditch, as with ditch I. Although we have no definite evidence, ditches I and II appear to have been converging on the southwest corner of the small enclosure of Alfred's Castle. The line of these ditches was made use of in constructing the enclosure, although the enclosure ditch, ditch V, enlarged the existing linears. Alfred's Castle may have been constructed at a point in the landscape already picked out as significant by the meeting of two linears.

Cut partially into the fill of ditch I and slightly to one side of it was a smaller V-shaped ditch (ditch IV), approximately 1 meter deep and recut at least once, following the line of the linear ditch toward the small enclosure. Ditch IV was dug after ditch I had fully silted up and could only have formed an ephemeral mark on the landscape. Trench 10 contained an indication of a possible ring ditch of an earlier barrow cut by ditch IV, and it may have been that the late Bronze Age linear (ditch I) had been aligned on an earlier barrow at this point.

On the eastern side of the site in area A a series of trenches was dug to reveal two and sometimes three ditches—called collectively ditch III. At some points these were separate and sometimes they cut each other, suggesting a number of phases of cutting, silting, and recutting of ditches. The ditches were aligned on an earlier round barrow, partially excavated by us, before turning sharply west along the modern fence line to join with the enclosure ditch of Alfred's Castle at its northernmost corner. At several points along the ditches early Iron Age pottery was recovered, suggesting that ditch(es) III were broadly contemporary with the digging of the Alfred's Castle enclosure ditch, which post-dates the linear ditches (I and II).

We thus have the following sequence, the earliest phases of which are somewhat speculative, the later phases much more certain. The earliest features on this site were round barrows, two of which may have been discovered through excavation and a third is suspected from aerial photographic evidence. One of these barrows may have been used to align the linear (ditch I) which came in from the north and the other for the later V-shaped ditches which form the eastern boundary of the large enclosure, ditch III. The Alfred's Castle enclosure was created at the point where two linears intersect and was broadly contemporary with the V-shaped ditches forming the large enclosure. The enclosure of Alfred's Castle itself was created through digging a V-shaped ditch, similar in profile to those mentioned above, but much deeper and steeper. Contemporary with this ditch was dense occupation of the interior, evidenced by one possible house structure and a mass of pits and other features. The pits contained rich assemblages of bronze and iron work, pottery, spindles whorls, loom weights, and animal bones dating from the early and the middle Iron Ages.

The structure of the rampart and the nature of the entrances into Alfred's Castle were explored through trenches 1 and 4. Trench 4 showed the break in the rampart on the western side of the enclosure was an original entrance and the rampart here was in two phases, with an original sarsen-faced rampart being supplemented by a substantial chalk bank with revetting posts. There is a break in the ditch in front of the gap in the rampart allowing movement in and out of the small enclosure and connecting with the large enclosure. The northwestern end of trench 1 showed that the rampart here was substantially different in character and may have been only of a single phase. It also demonstrated that the break in the rampart was not original but had been made in the Romano-British period with Romano-British pottery, hobnails, and other artifacts in the upper fills of the ditch, together with substantial amounts of sarsen stones, probably pushed down from the rampart to form a consolidated surface.

Pits and postholes within the enclosure in trench 1 were also filled with Romano-British material. This activity is related to the building and use of a Romano-British villa house which was constructed inside the small enclosure in the late 1st century CE, thus continuing links to the past and extending the sequence of the site into the 3rd century CE when the building was abandoned. Despite the name Alfred's Castle, there is no evidence of post-Roman activity at the site.

The main evidence of Romano-British occupation of Alfred's Castle is a stone building in the center of the enclosure (Figure 2.2). This building was excavated over two seasons. Excavations revealed the building to be relatively small and centrally located within the enclosure and of a type which might best be described as a "villa house" (Henig and Booth 2000:82, fig. 4.2). The building was made up of six rooms, five of which were probably constructed in the late 1st or early 2nd centuries and the final one, at the southwestern end, was a later addition, probably in the 3rd century, not long before the building was allowed to collapse.

Walls 2005 and 2008 were constructed later than the outer walls, to form new rooms, but probably are not much later in date. The building lacked a corridor, although it is just possible that it was originally an ailsed building, with internal divisions created slightly later in its history. Two large sarsens at either ends of wall 2008 might have formed supports for the bases of posts.

Wall plaster and window glass were recovered, but there was no trace of a mosaic pavement or a hypocaust, indicating that although the building was a substantial stone structure, it was not especially rich or well-appointed.

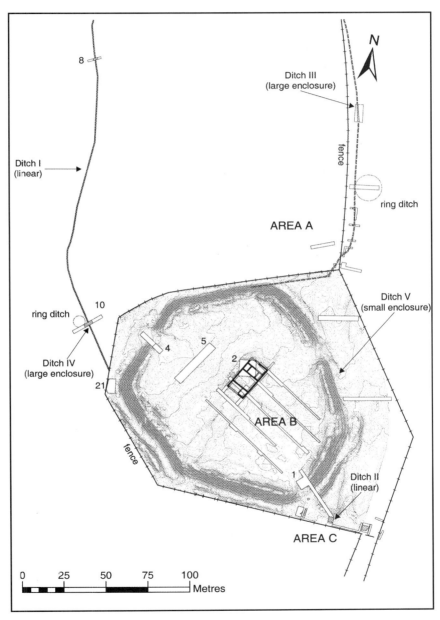

Figure 2.2 Plan of Alfred's Castle.

There were a mass of Iron Age pits and other features under the villa house, and where walls had been laid over pits their tops had been filled with sarsen packing, indicating an awareness of the earlier features on the site on the part of the later inhabitants.

A number of ancillary structures was found in the area around the house, made of sarsen and tile, some of which exhibited evidence of craft and agricultural activities, such as a crucible found in sarsen structure at the northern end of trench 5. The villa house represented a local center of the agricultural economy, as well as linking into the wider Roman world through buying a range of artifacts from both local and more distant parts of the Roman Empire.

In summary, the site of Alfred's Castle provides evidence of long-term, if discontinuous, use. From the alignment of late Bronze linear ditches and early Iron Age V-shaped ditches on earlier Bronze Age round barrows and the construction of the enclosure of Alfred's Castle along the line of two linear ditches, the creators of the site have showed considerable awareness of the past. This awareness continued into the Romano-British period with the construction of a substantial stone building in the middle of the enclosure, the creation of a break through the rampart, and the filling in of the enclosure ditch to create a new entrance. The new stone house, although modest by the more general standards of Roman Britain, would have been an obvious and visible statement on the Berkshire Downs and we feel that it is no coincidence that this statement was made within an earlier enclosure. Just as there was a break in time between the construction of round barrows and the digging of the linear ditch, so there was a gap between the early and middle Iron Age occupation of the Alfred's Castle enclosure and the late 1st century CE building. This discontinuity makes the link with the past that the building signalled more intriguing rather than less.

The material world is an important source of emotions, and the values we attach to people cannot be understood without looking at the values deriving from the things that were important to them. Repeated actions and links to the past through memory or myth evoke emotions linking childhood experiences to the world of the present. The digging of ditches in late prehistory might seem mundane and utilitarian acts to us but could have been an important element of peoples' emotional anchors to the world. Linking older ditch systems to newer ones through the last millennium BCE made claims on the past by those in the present. The wholesale re-attachment of people to things that took place as Romanization unfolded was profound, if not sudden or imposed. The fact that, in the case of Alfred's Castle, new ways were adopted within a context where links to the past could be maintained and emphasized is surely important. The building of a villa-house, probably the first in this area of rural Britannia, was not just a statement made in stone of a new commitment to rectangular form, but the center of new forms of commensualism and community. Food and drink of novel types were consumed from fine and coarse pottery, both imported from long distances and made relatively locally. Window glass, coinage, and bronzes all indicate a new shape, quality, and dynamic to human relationships. The new villa was built on an old site. The builders were not breaking with their past, but reshaping it. Maybe they used links to Iron Age ancestry to damp down the novelty of what they did and to deflect criticisms that attach to the nouveau riche. Maybe the imposition of a rectangular form on a round one emphasized the daring nature of what they attempted. Maybe claims to Iron Age ancestry were fictive, or never made. We cannot know.

But we can see that conscious choice was being exercised, so the new qualities attached to life were nuanced through being surrounded by ancient marks on the landscape. Links with the past had little to do with quantity, as it is very unlikely that any reliable dated accounts existed of the earlier history of Alfred's Castle, stretching as it did back a thousand years and more before the construction of the villa. But the qualities of claims on the present made through links to the past were vital, reinforcing the earlier point that we do not pass through time; time passes through us.

References

Bourdieu, Pierre. *The Logic of Practice*. Cambridge: Polity Press, 1990.

Carsten, Janet, ed. *The Cultures of Relatedness. New Approaches to the Study of Kinship*. Cambridge: Cambridge University Press, 2000.

Gell, Alfred. *The Anthropology of Time: Cultural Constructions of Temporal Maps and Images*. Oxford: Berg, 1992.

Gosden, Chris. *Social Being and Time*. Oxford: Blackwell, 1994.

———. "Making sense: Archaeology and Aesthetics." *World Archaeology* 33 (2000):163–67.

Henig, Martin, and Paul Booth. *Roman Oxfordshire*. Stroud: Sutton, 2000.

Ingold, Tim. "The Temporality of Landscape." *World Archaeology* 25 (1993):152–73.

Nussbaum, Martha C. *Upheavals of Thought. The Intelligence of the Emotions*. Cambridge: Cambridge University Press, 2000.

Reddy, William M. *The Navigation of Feeling. A Framework for the History of the Emotions*. Cambridge: Cambridge University Press, 2001.

Sharples, Niall M. *Maiden Castle: Excavations and Field Survey 1985–6*. London: English Heritage Archaeological Report 19, 1991.

Woolf, Greg. "Beyond Romans and Natives." *World Archaeology* 28 (1997):339–50.

———. *Becoming Roman in Gaul. The Origins of Provincial Civilization in Gaul*. Cambridge: Cambridge University Press, 1998.

• • 3 • •

SCHOLARLY CONCEPTIONS AND QUANTIFICATIONS OF TIME IN ASSYRIA AND BABYLONIA, C.750–250 BCE

Eleanor Robson

We owe many basic concepts and quantifications of time, from the twelve-month year to the sixty-second minute, to the scholars of ancient Iraq. My aim here is not to recount the teleological story of how those ideas moved through time and space from them to us, but rather to explore time as it is represented in scholarly writings of all sorts in the historical record. I shall focus primarily on two bodies of evidence: one from the cities of Ashur, Kalhu, and Nineveh, successive capitals of Assyria—northern Iraq, in the region of modern-day Mosul—from about 750 to 612 BCE; and the other from the Babylonian cities of Babylon and Uruk, to the south of Baghdad, in around 500–250 BCE.

Assyria in the mid-8th to late 7th centuries was at the height of its imperial power. It controlled almost all of the Middle East (including Egypt for two short periods), from which it earned phenomenal income, in both taxation and war booty. Much of that wealth was invested in the upkeep, expansion, and replacement of three urban centres in its heartland on the Tigris River. First and foremost was Ashur, the historic religious and cultural capital of the empire, after which its tutelary deity was named. In 879 BCE king Ashurnasirpal II moved the political capital north to Kalhu, and just before 700 Sennacherib relocated to Nineveh. Before these cities fell to the Medes and the Babylonians as the empire collapsed in 614–612 BCE all three were the focus of lavish spending, particularly on their temples and palaces—and on the personnel attached to those institutions.

The Assyrian court comprised not only political and military officials and advisers but also men of learning, *ummanu*, whose fields of expertise were vast, ranging from religion to science, from medicine to magic. These elite literati depended almost entirely, it seems, on royal patronage to keep them in housing and employment, creating a highly competitive atmosphere which drove intellectual innovation as they fought among themselves for preferment. As the rulers were particularly concerned with determining the gods' will by means of terrestrial and celestial omens, there were especially strong motives to improve the predictability of key celestial events (Leichty 1993; Brown 2000a:33–52). Lunar and solar eclipses were particularly portentous for king and country. The scholars of celestial omens held the title *tupshar enuma anu ellil* ("scribe of 'When the gods Anu and Ellil'"), after the first line of the major compilation of omens, which ran to 70 or more tablets and is so vast that it still has not been published in its entirety (Rochberg 2000; Hunger and Pingree 1999:12–20, 32–50).

The sudden destruction of the scholars' homes and workplaces has left us with their personal and official libraries of scholarly works—some newly composed, some carefully copied from ancient originals, some recast or commented upon (Pedersén 1998:132–65). They range from historical and historiographical works to literary and mythological compositions, from hymns and ritual instructions to medical and astronomical compendia. The palaces have also yielded their reports to, and correspondence with, their kingly patrons, giving unparalleled opportunities to compare the written tradition with day-to-day praxis (Starr 1990; Hunger 1992; Parpola 1993; Cole and Machinist 1998).

All that comes down to us was written on clay tablets using the highly complex cuneiform script, in the languages of Akkadian (an indirect relative of Hebrew and Arabic) and Sumerian (which has no known linguistic relatives). This cluster of writing practices had been in use since the first urbanization of Iraq in the late 4th millennium BCE, but they were by now on their way out of both spoken and written currency. Aramaic, which was rapidly replacing them, had the massive communicative advantage of an alphabetic script, but from our perspective the insuperable disadvantage of perishable media. Clay tablets, however, survive in the hundreds of thousands—probably millions—so we are fortunate indeed that ancient scholars continued to employ the traditional medium of cuneiform scholarship.

The Assyrians may have considered themselves rulers of the known universe but they were very conscious of their cultural dependence on their southern neighbor Babylonia, from which almost all of their traditions, writings, and belief systems ultimately stemmed. At times the Assyrian kings even ordered raids on Babylonian libraries, bringing back cultural booty in the form of cuneiform tablets and Babylonian scribes in fetters (Michalowski 1999). Thus much of the contents of Assyrian scholarship was essentially Babylonian.

The scholarly tradition seems to have been relatively unaffected by the major political reconfigurations of the 610s and even survived the Persian and Seleucid conquests of 539 and 330 BCE more or less unscathed. This may have been because the Assyrian system of court patronage had never extended to Babylonia, where scholars were dependent on the stable institution of the city temple rather than the fickle support of the current king. Indeed, scholarly activity appears to have continued regardless of who was in power: the will of the gods needed to be determined for the good of the land, whatever the political circumstances.

From about 500 BCE onward scholarship at Marduk's temple Esangila in Babylon and at Resh, the sanctuary of the sky-god Anu in Uruk, was increasingly focused toward ever more sophisticated mathematical methods for modelling celestial periodicities so ominous phenomena were completely predictable (Rochberg 1993). Just as earlier in Assyria, cuneiform scholarship was in the hands of a few families of wealthy urbanites, who trained their own sons and the sons of professional colleagues, who all traced their ancestry back to famous scholars of centuries ago. While the title *tupshar enuma anu ellil* was still used occasionally, the preferred professional designations, which ran along familial lines, were *ashipu* ("incantation priest") and *kalu* ("lamentation priest"). In 3rd century Uruk two families most heavily involved in quantitative methods of celestial prediction were the Ekur-zakir family of *ashipus*, and the Sin-leqi-unninni family of *kalus*. The latter group even claimed descent from the late 2nd millennium editor of the *Epic of Gilgamesh* (Beaulieu 2000). Cuneiform scholars were still active in Babylon in the 1st century CE, and perhaps even two centuries after that (Sachs 1976; Geller 1997).

How did the scholars of ancient Babylonia and Assyria conceptualize the past, present, and future of their land? How did they perceive the flow of time? Historians of astronomy have typically depicted them as the first rational scientists of the Western tradition, observing, quantifying, recording, and classifying in order to build sophisticated mathematical models of time on a sound empirical base. Philologists and literary historians, on the other hand, have tended to focus on ancient constructions of the distant and genealogical past. These apparently mutually exclusive concerns are more a reflection of the narrow focus of each of Snow's "two cultures" of modern scholarship—the scientific and the humanistic—than of any ancient reality (Snow 1959). The elite literati of Assyria and Babylonia were the numerati too, and their writings show a much richer, more complex, and at times confusing and contradictory, understanding of time and temporality than earlier studies have allowed. The approach adopted here may appear eclectic but it simply attempts to replicate the wide-ranging interests of the ancients themselves.

Reconciling Real and Ideal Time

The great Epic of Creation *enuma elish* ("When Above") was recited on the fourth day of the *akitu*, or equinoctial festival, held on the eleven days after the first new moon of the spring equinox at the beginning of the year (Bidmead 2002). At the city of Uruk during the Seleucid period it was held at the autumnal equinox, the midpoint of the year. In Babylonia the god Marduk was both the focal point of the festival and the hero and sole audience of the epic; in Assyria it was Ashur. The equinoctial recital of the *Epic* was not only a marker of passing time; it both described and initiated "the irruption of primordial—and hence dangerous or sacred—time in to mundane time, an irruption that both threaten[ed] and enriche[d] the cosmic order" (Sommer 2000:82). For on the day of the *akitu* following its performance, Marduk's temple Esangila was ritually destroyed, purified, and rebuilt, symbolizing the abolition and renewal of the whole cosmic order, with the person of the king at its center, after which the king's right to rule was reaffirmed by Marduk (or Ashur) himself.

The *Epic* describes the creation of the world of the gods, in which time passes unquantified, and the hero god's destruction of the forces of chaos and evil in the form of the monstrous sea Tiamat. From her lifeless body he creates the world in which human beings are to dwell. Thus chaos is always immanent in the world, a constant counter-force to the orderliness imposed by Marduk. In the sky he positions the heavenly bodies and sets them in regular motion to define and structure the year:

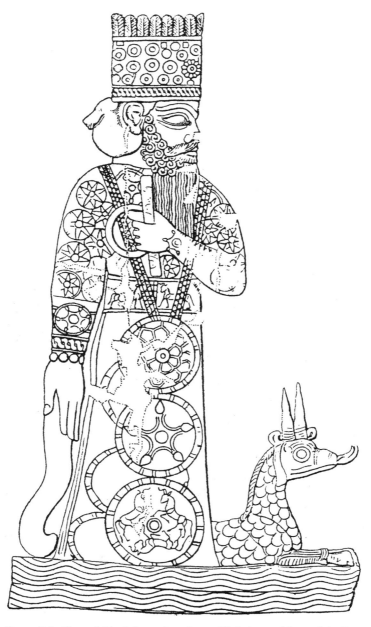

Figure 3.1 The god Marduk, tutelary deity of Babylon and hero of the Epic of Creation, *with his snake-dragon. The image is from the god's own cylinder seal, carved from lapis lazuli and dedicated to him by a Babylonian king of the 9th century BCE. From* F. H. Weissbach, Babylonische Miscellen. Leipzig: Hinrichs, 1903, *fig. 1.*

[Marduk] made the positions for the great gods.
He set up the stars in constellations, their counterparts.
He designated the year and marked out its divisions,
Apportioned three stars each to twelve months.
After he had patterned the days of the year,
He fixed the position of the Pole Star to mark out their courses,
So that none of them could go wrong or stray.
He fixed the positions of Ellil and Ea together with it.
(Tablet V:1–7; cf. Dalley 1989:255)

In other words, every one of the gods is represented in the sky by a star. The stars are to rotate around the Pole Star—as indeed they appear to do. Because for most of the northern hemisphere of the earth's surface the Pole Star is not directly overhead, the stars that are nearest to it are always visible in the night sky throughout the year, while the band of stars further away appear to rise and set over the year, and there is another group, of southern circumpolar stars, which are never visible in the northern night sky. Marduk chooses 36 of those stars in the middle band as chronological markers, three of which are to rise in each month.

The evidence for this interpretation, which otherwise might appear to be an over-reading of the *Epic*, comes from a genre of scholarly compositions dating to the 1180s BCE and later, whose ancient title was "Three Stars Each"—notice the intertextuality—but are now more prosaically (and erroneously, for they are not navigation aids) called "Astrolabes." They consist of a month-by-month listing, or sometimes a circular pictorial representation, of constellations, stars, and planets which make their first appearance, or heliacal rising, on the eastern horizon in each of the 12 30-day months of the ideal calendar (of which more below). The horizon is divided into three sectors for this purpose: the Path of Anu the sky-god (a band of about 35° around due east); the Path of Ea, god of wisdom (to the south of the Path of Anu); and the

Path of Ellil, father of the gods (to the north of Path of Anu). Each "astrolabe" assigns a slightly different group of stars to each Path (an example is given in Table 3.1).

Later astronomical works built upon this scheme, including the widely attested two-tablet compilation of celestial information now known as MUL.APIN ("Plough Star"), which reached its final form by about 700 BCE but was still copied for centuries after that (Hunger and Pingree 1989:271–77). We also see Marduk closely associated with the Pole Star throughout the scholarly tradition, for instance in Astrolabe B: "the red star which stands at the rising of the south wind after the gods of the night have finished their duties and divides the heavens: this star is the Pole Star, Marduk" (section B, ii, 29–32; Horowitz 1998:159).

Marduk's next act in the *Epic of Creation* is to create the moon, giving it detailed instructions on how to demarcate the lunar month:

> He made the crescent moon appear, entrusted night (to it)
> And designated it the jewel of the night to mark out the days.
>
> "Go forth every month without fail as a crescent disc,
> At the beginning of the month, to wax over the land.
> You shall shine with horns to mark out six days;
> On the seventh day the disc shall be half.
> On the fifteenth day you shall always be in opposition, at the mid-point of each month.
> When the sun faces you from the horizon of heaven,
> Wane at the same pace and form in reverse.
> Always begin the day of disappearance close to the path of the sun,
> And on the [. . .] of the thirtieth day you shall be in conjunction with the sun a second time."
> (Tablet V:12–22; cf. Dalley 1989:256)

TABLE 3.1 THE RISING STARS OF ASTROLABE B

Month		Path of Ea	Path of Anu	Path of Ellil
I	Nisannu	Field	Venus	Plough
II	Ayyaru	Stars	Scorpion	Annunitu
III	Simanu	Jaw of the Bull	Scales	Snake
IV	Du'uzu	True Shepherd of Anu	Panther	Wagon
V	Abu	Arrow	Old Man	[...]
VI	Ululu	Bow	Swallow	She-goat
VII	Tashritu	The City of Eridu	[Lion]	Wolf
VIII	Arahsamnu	Great Lady	[Twins]	Eagle
IX	Kislimu	Mad Dog	Great Twins	Pig
X	Tebetu	Mars	Crab	Jupiter
XI	Shabatu	Habasiranu	Raven	Fox
XII	Addaru	Fish	Pole Star	Southern Yoke

Sources: Astrolabe B, VAT 9416 (KAV 218), section B. The most recent discussion of "astrolabes" is Hunger and Pingree (1999:50–63); see also Horowitz (1998:154–66). For identifications of constellations and star names, see Hunger and Pingree (1989:271–77).

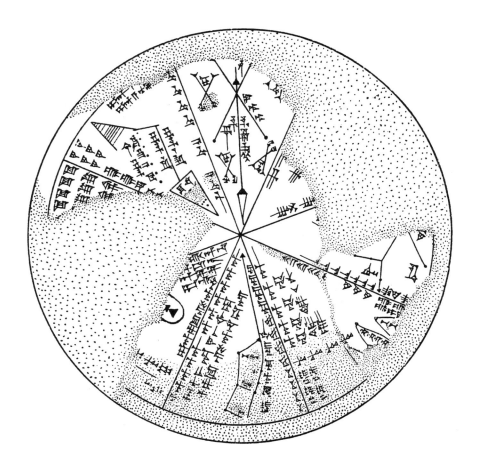

Figure 3.2 A circular star map from Nineveh dividing the night sky into eight and illustrating the most prominent constellations. From L.W. King, Cuneiform Texts from Babylonian Tablets, &c., in the British Museum 33. London: Trustees of the British Museum, 1912, pl. 10.

Only after he has set time in motion does Marduk create the natural world itself and then mankind (Tablets V and VI; cf. Dalley 1989:255–67).

The *Epic of Creation* embodies two conflicting ways of marking present time: Marduk orders to the moon and the "three stars each" to operate an ideal calendar of twelve 30-day months, making a year of 360 days. But the real lunar calendar—in which each day began at sunset, the start of each month was designated by the first sighting of the new moon 29 or 30 nights since the last one, and the year started with the new moon after the spring equinox—averages just 354 days. And of course the solar year, at 365 1/4 days, is longer than either. It was a major scholarly endeavor to keep the lunar calendar in line with the solar year and to reconcile them both to the ideal year that the gods had decreed. Shortfalls in the real calendar were seen as a divine indicator of the real world's shortcomings in attaining godly standards of perfection. But the ideal calendar was not only understood to have been divinely ordained by the god Marduk: it was also administratively convenient. Temple records from the city of Uruk in the late 4th millennium BCE are already witness to a 360-day year of 12 30-day months, and this remained the accounting norm throughout the 3rd millennium and beyond (Englund 1988; 1991).

However, in reality about a half of the months of the year were only 29 days long: in Babylonian parlance the first day of the month was *turru* (turned back) instead of *kunnu* (firm) as it should have been. Assyrian and Babylonian scholars expended much energy and ingenuity in predicting month lengths, as witnessed by reports to kings as well as collections of prediction rules (Brack-Bernsen 2002). Thirty-day months were considered much more auspicious than their 29-day counterparts, as can be seen in the omens which scholars to the Assyrian court typically associated with sightings of the new moon (Beaulieu 1993). Compare the chief scribe Issar-shumu-eresh's upbeat assessment for a new month after 30 days: "If the moon becomes visible on the 1st day: reliable speech; the land will become happy," with his more cautionary "If the moon becomes visible on the 30th day: there will be frost, variant: rumour of the enemy" (Hunger 1992:10–11).

Babylonian temples too needed to adjust their cultic cycle, moving clothing ceremonies and animal sacrifices forward or backward a day according to the length of the month (Beaulieu 1993; Robbins 1996). Here, for instance, is a priest of the sun-god Shamash in the 6th century city of Larsa writing to his superior ("father") at Eana in nearby Uruk: "Tablet of Shamash-idri to the administrator my father. May Shamash and Bunene decree the well-being and health of my father. We heard the report concerning the turning-back of the (first) day. Shamash will be clothed on the 15th day (intead of the 14th). May the lord send whatever (is needed) for (that) day. May the lord (also) send a weaver and a clothes-washer" (NCBT 58; Beaulieu 1993:77–78).

It was imperative that the temples retain the ideal calendrical cycle of the gods in the face of the vagaries of real-world lunation and that meant maintaining the rhythms of ritual whatever the profane reality.

Eleven days difference between the lunar and solar year also required regular readjustment to keep the months in line with the seasons and the new year in line with the spring equinox. Intercalation, or addition of an extra month after the sixth or twelfth month, was for most of Assyrian and Babylonian history carried out on an *ad hoc* basis, by royal proclamation following scholarly advice. Here the *tupshar enuma anu ellil* Balasi advises king Esarhaddon in early 670 BCE on the need to intercalate: "Concerning the adding of the intercalary month about which the king my lord wrote to me, this is indeed an intercalary year. After Jupiter has become visible I shall write again to the king my lord. I am waiting for it, but it will take the whole month. Then we shall see how it is and when we have to add the intercalary month" (Parpola 1993:42).

The astronomical compendium *MUL.APIN* contains two simple schemes for intercalation, based on observing celestial phenomena which should theoretically occur on or near fixed dates in the ideal calendar, and adding an extra month when those phenomena occur a month too late, as Balasi describes (Hunger and Pingree 1999:75–79). This unnamed Assyrian king, probably also Esarhaddon, sends out notices to his provincial governors, presumably at his scholars' behest: "Order of the king to Zeruti (the city governor) and to the clergy of the city of Der. I am well; you may be content. Be informed that there will be an intercalary Addaru (Month XII). Perform the festival and rites of my gods in a favorable month" (Cole and Machinist 1998:4).

In the late 6th century intercalation became regulated not by royal proclamation but by the close observation of lunar periodicity. Starting in 527 BCE, during the reign of the Persian king Cambyses, there were three successive eight-year intercalation cycles to bring the spring equinox back into Addaru (Month XII) instead of Nisannu (Month I), before the adoption in 503 BCE of a fixed pattern of seven intercalary months every nineteen years, which is often erroneously named after Meton of Athens, fl. c.450 BCE (Britton 1993:66–68; Bowen and Goldstein 1988). The emerging understanding of the precise relationship between days, months, and years in 1st millennium Babylonia is surveyed by Britton (2002).

Babylonian chronology was based on regnal years. For instance when the trainee *ashipu* Anu-aba-usur copied a commentary on lunar eclipses from *enuma anu ellil* Tablet 20 for his father Iqisha he dated it "Uruk, Ululu (Month X) day 3, year 2 of Philip, king of the lands" (322 BCE) (W 22330; von Weiher 1983–98:IV,162). If, as was often the case, a new ruler came to the throne midyear, that accession year continued to be named after the previous king, and for dating purposes the new reign was deemed to start on the following New Year's Day.

It was not until the late 4th century BCE that a continuous dating system was invented, which would allow future years to be named and counted. The Seleucid Era officially began retrospectively on New Year's Day of the first regnal year of Seleucus I Nicator (3

April 311 BCE); year names now took the form "Year 97, Antiochus was king (214–3 BCE)" (Hunger and Pingree 1999:xiii). The 19-year intercalation cycle continued to be used. The units and arithmetical models with which the scholars measured the passing of time are well understood (Brown 2000b; Hunger 2001) even if the physical means by which they did so are not (Brown et al. 1999–2000; Fermor and Steele 2000).

Constructing the Past, Present, and Future

The distinction between the sacred, timeless past and quantifiable, historical time was not limited to the particular context of the *akitu* festival. It was also occasionally marked, for instance, in royal foundation inscriptions which kings had ceremonially buried in the walls of temples whose renovations they had sponsored. When in 679 BCE Esarhaddon, king of Assyria, commissioned the rebuilding of E-sharra, the god Ashur's temple in the city of Ashur, he also acknowledged the reconstruction work of earlier kings:

> Ashur's ancient temple, which Ushpia my (fore)father, Ashur's high-priest, had previously built, and which had become dilapidated, and which Erishum, son of Ilu-shumma, my (fore)father, Ashur's high priest rebuilt: 126 years passed and it returned to dilapidation, and Shamshi-Adad, son of Ilu-kabkabbi, my (fore)father, Ashur's high priest, rebuilt it. 434 years passed and that temple was destroyed by fire. Shalmaneser, son of Adad-Nirari, my (fore)father, Ashur's high priest, rebuilt it. 580 years passed and the interior shrine, dwelling of Ashur my lord, the summit building, the shrine of the *kubu* images, the astral deities' shrine, the god Ea's shrine, had become worn out, dilapidated, and old. (Ass A, III:16–41; Borger 1956:1–6)

It happens that Esarhaddon's 13th century predecessor Shalmaneser I also left five different versions of a foundation inscription within the temple precinct and elsewhere in the city (Grayson 1987:109–237, A.0.77.1–5). Esarhaddon's history (one surviving exemplar of which even imitates it in deliberately archaizing script) is an almost word-for-word copy of one of them:

> When E-hursang-kurkura, the ancient temple, which Ushpia, my (fore)father, Ashur's high priest, had previously built and which had become dilapidated, and which Erishum, my (fore)father, Ashur's high priest, rebuilt: 159 years passed and that temple returned to dilapidation, and Shamshi-Adad, also my (fore)father, Ashur's high priest rebuilt it. 580 years passed and the temple and its sanctuary were destroyed by fire. . . . I deposited my monumental inscriptions and foundation documents. He who alters my inscriptions and my name: may Ashur, my lord, overturn his kingship and eradicate his name and his seed from the land. (Grayson 1987:189 A.0.77.2 5–13, 21–24)

Esarhaddon's only non-trivial emendations to Shalmaneser's text are the addition of his predecessors' patronyms and the alteration of the time spans between them (Table 3.2).

Assyrian court scribes were able to assign exact spans of time to the past thanks to their system of naming each year after a *limmu*, or eponym official, who was chosen annually according to his status in the court hierarchy (Finkel and Reade 1995). The date at the bottom of one copy of Esarhaddon's foundation inscription, for instance, reads "Du'uzu (Month IV), day 19. Eponymy of Itti-Adad-aninu" (679 BCE). Lists of these *limmus* were maintained for administrative purposes, and in addition *limmu* officials often commemorated their year of office by setting up stele by the side of the monumental roadway into the city of Ashur.

TABLE 3.2 TIME SPANS BETWEEN REBUILDING OF ASHUR'S TEMPLE ACCORDING TO
FOUNDATION INSCRIPTIONS OF SHALMANESER I AND ESARHADDON

Time span	Shalmaneser's Inscription	Esarhaddon's Inscription	Assyrian King List	Modern Maximum	Modern Minimum
Ushpia (regnal dates unknown) – Erishum (1939–1900)	uncounted	uncounted	uncounted	—	—
Erishum (1939–1900) – Shamshi-Adad (1813–1781)	159	126	[5 reigns]	158	87
Shalmaneser (1273–1244) – Shamshi-Adad (1813–1781)	580	434	421 [+ 2 reigns]	569	508
Shamshi-Adad (1813–1781) – Esarhaddon (680–669: 679)	—	580	523 (+ 42)	594	565

Limmu lists are completely reconstructible as far back as 910 BCE and fragmentarily attested for two hundred years before that (Millard 1994), while the so-called *Assyrian King List* records the names and lengths of reign of kings of Ashur going right back to the early 2nd millennium BCE and the days of "17 kings who lived in tents" (Grayson 1980). The King List, whose three best-preserved exemplars end with the reigns of Tiglath-pileser II (966–935 BCE), Ashur-nirari V (754–745 BCE), and Shalmaneser V (726–722 BCE), respectively, was compiled wherever possible from *limmu* lists; it describes one group of early rulers as "total of 6 kings [whose names occur on (?)] bricks, whose eponyms are destroyed." According to modern chronology Shalmaneser's time spans (159 years, 580 years) are much closer to modern consensus than Esarhaddon's revisions of them (126 years, 434 years). The second of those, however, appears to be based on the *Assyrian King List*, composed on present evidence some three centuries after Shalmaneser's reign. It gives the total time span between Shamshi-Adad I and Shalmaneser I as 421 years and 1 month plus the reigns of two kings whose lengths are missing from the extant exemplars. Esarhaddon's scholars, then, seem to have put more weight on their own evidence-based quantifications of the past than on the authority of ancient writings and were capable of rewriting the historical record accordingly.

No temporal quantifications are attached to the temple's supposed founder, Ushpia, who has left no traces whatsoever in the archaeological or historical record except as the penultimate entry in the enumeration of the "17 kings who lived in tents" at the start of the *Assyrian King List* (Harper et al. 1995:37). The building inscriptions of neither Erishum (Grayson 1987:19–37, A.0.33.1–14) nor Shamshi-Adad I (Grayson 1987:47–63, A.0.39.1,9,11) mention any royal builder earlier than Erishum himself. Shalmaneser's scholars appear to have added Ushpia to the beginning architectural genealogy, as an attested king from the primordial time before the quantifiable past, in order to imbue the temple with deep antiquity (Robson 2001).

Figure 3.3 The seven antediluvian sages were thought to have been half man, half fish. This bas-relief was erected in the temple of Ninurta in Kalhu, c. 875 BCE, and is now in the British Museum. Photograph by the author.

Scholarship itself was deemed to have been bequeathed to mankind in the primordial past. Mesopotamian spells and incantations "creat[es] magic by harking back to a primeval time" (Livingstone 1999:131). And according to the late 2nd millennium *Myth of Adapa* and other sources, Ea, the god of wisdom, sent seven semi-divine sages to the antediluvian city of Eridu in order "to disclose the design of the land" (line 2; Dalley 1989:184). Esarhaddon's son Ashurbanipal (668–27 BCE) recalls this tradition in one of his own self-laudatory royal inscriptions:

> I have learnt the skill of Adapa the sage, secret knowledge of
>   the entire scribal craft;
> I observe and discuss celestial and terrestrial omens in the
>   meetings of scholars;
> With expert diviners I interpret the liver, the mirror of heaven;
> I solve difficult reciprocals and multiplications lacking clear solution;
> I have read elaborate texts in obscure Sumerian and
>   Akkadian which is difficult to interpret;
> I examine stone inscriptions from the time before the Flood.
> (L4 I 13–18; Streck 1916:254–6)

Thus distant antiquity was inherent in the concept of scholarship itself.

As Esarhaddon implies in his account of the reconstruction of Ashur's temple, there were considered to be ideal times for certain activities, and conversely ill-favored moments: "I felt danger, I was afraid. I was negligent in renewing that temple. In the diviners' wooden bowl the gods Shamash and Adad answered me a true yes: they caused an omen to be written on a sheep's liver for building that temple, for the renewal of its inner sanctum" (Ass A III.42–IV.6; Borger 1956:3).

Esarhaddon requests his diviners to ritually induce an ominous sign from the gods in the innards of a sacrificial sheep, confirming divine consent to his plans. But he could also have asked them to

Figure 3.4 A baru *inspects the entrails of a the sacrificial ram, depicted on a bas-relief from Ashurnasirpal II's palace at Kalhu, c. 875 BCE, now in the British Museum. Photograph by the author.*

TABLE 3.3 FAVORABLE, UNFAVORABLE, AND DANGEROUS
OR EVIL DAYS OF THE MONTH OF DU'UZU

Day	Ashur hemerology	Nineveh-Babylon hemerology
7	Outbreak of fire	Favorable day in the house: favorable for the slave
18	Favorable for the [slave] in his master's house	Terror: hostility on the road
19	Favorable for the king	Favorable for the king
20	Unfavorable	Unfavorable
21	[. . .]	Favorable for the king

consult a hemerology, or ominous calendar. Many different hemerologies are known, from the mid-2nd millennium BCE to the Seleucid Period, enumerating the favorable (*magru*), unfavorable (*la magru*), and dangerous or evil (*lemnu*) days of the ideal year for carrying out particular activities, in patterns which vary slightly from city to city according to local belief systems and traditions of transmission (Labat 1939:40). Compare these two calendrically organized hemerologies for the days around 19 Du'uzu (Month IV), on which the building inscription was written (see Table 3.3). The first is from Ashur (Labat 1939) and the second known in copies from Nineveh and Babylon (Labat 1941:24), but according to both of them 19 Du'uzu was a day deemed to be "favorable for the king."

There seems to have been general agreement between the 1st millennium hemerologies, with the second half of the year being most favorable, with an average of 16 favorable days a month compared to 11 in the first half. Neither are the gods' good graces spread evenly across the months: the 3rd day of the month was favorable only twice a year, while the 1st, 15th, and 22nd of the month were each favorable in 9 months out of 12 (Labat 1941:20–21). These 3 days are closely linked to the ideal lunar cycle as decreed by Marduk in the *Epic of Creation*. The Assyrian royal hemerology is even called *enbu bel arhi* ("New Moon, Lord of the Month").

Independent of a day's favorable or unfavorable aspect was its dangerous or evil character, which was unchanging from month to month. Early hemerologies counted 9 unfavorable days a month, but by the period we are dealing with there were just 5: the 7th, 14th, 19th, 21st, and 28th. On these days almost all activity was forbidden by the gods, except those relating to mourning and penitence (Labat 1939:44). It is striking that 4 of the 5 days are multiples of 7, and can once again be related to the key moments of the lunar cycle: the day before the full moon, the day before disappearance, and the 2 half-way points in between. It has also been suggested that the 19th day acquired its dangerous character from that fact that it is $7 \times 7 = 49$ days since the last new moon (Labat 1939:45). In the Nineveh-Babylon hemerology mentioned above, there were no favorable yet dangerous days in the months of Simanu (Month III) and Abu (Month V), yet in Tashritu (Month VII) and Shabatu (Month XI) all the dangerous days were considered favorable. On average two or three days a month were both favorable and dangerous at the same time.

Although no edition of *enbu bel arhi* has yet been published (see Landsberger 1915; Livingstone 1999:137), there is a contemporary royal menology, or list of ominous months for kingly activity, which bore the title *iqqur ipush* ("He Destroyed, He Built"). It exists in two different versions, one ordered primarily by activity, the other taking that same material and reordering it by month (Labat 1965). Interestingly in the light of Esarhaddon's concern over Ashur's temple, the first 33 sections of the first version all concern the foundation and restoration of temples and cultic objects:

If in Nisannu (Month I) he builds a temple: its foundations
will not be stable
If in Ayyaru (Month II), ditto: he will see evil
If in Simanu (Month III), ditto: joy
If in Du'uzu (Month IV), ditto: his temple will last
If in Abu (Month V), ditto: his heart will be content.
(Labat 1965:63)

The section on Du'uzu (Month IV) in the version ordered by month has not survived, but it will have conveyed the same message: that Du'uzu is a favorable month for building.

It may simply be coincidence that Esarhaddon's building inscription was dated to a day deemed favorable for royal construction activities, but there is further evidence that menologies and hemerologies did not sit idle on the library shelves. Neo-Assyrian *barutu* (liver omen) rituals and reports were never performed and written on the days forbidden by *enbu bel arhi*, with just one exception. Outside the immediate cultic context of the royal court, the dates of contemporaneous legal documents from Nineveh, Kalhu, and Ashur do not follow the hemerologies so strictly. Nevertheless there seems to have been a clear preference for the 1st and 20th days of the month as propitious times to enter into contracts, and an avoidance of the 2nd, 8th, 19th, 24th, and 28th–30th days (Livingstone 1993).

Nearly twenty letters to Assyrian kings from their scholars attest to the regular use of menologies and hemerologies. Here the *tupshar enuma anu ellil* Nabu-ahhe-eriba writes to king Esarhaddon in Addaru (Month XII) of 670 BCE: "Concerning the arrangement of the banquet about which the king, my lord, wrote to me—(according to the menologies) 'If he wants to take the cult ceremonies'—it is favorable this month. It is favorable to arrange the banquet. Let them arrange it on the 13th, 15th, or the 17th day" (Parpola 1993:70).

In this letter the *ashipu* Nabu-nadin-shumi countermands the king's orders with the authority of the hemerologies behind him:

> Concerning the apotropaic *namburbu* ritual against evil of any kind, about which the king, my lord wrote to me, "Perform it tomorrow"—the day is not favorable. We shall prepare it on the 25th and perform it on the 26th.
>
> Anyway, the king, my lord, should not worry about this portent. The gods Bel (Marduk) and Nabu can make a portent pass by, and they will make it pass by the king, my lord. The king, my lord should not be afraid. (Parpola 1993:141)

The Assyrian king's life was thus shaped and controlled by the patterns of the ominous calendar. His actions were monitored, sanctioned, and temporally constrained by his scholars, who imposed their own individual readings of ominous portent on the person of the king and thereby on the state as a whole. But if there were thus limits to royal power, there were even greater restrictions on the scholars' influence over the king. There was intense competition between them for royal attention—Balasi and Nabu-ahhe-eriba were in particularly acrimonious dispute (Brown 2000a:240)—and the king could dispense with their services at will (Parpola 1987). As the second paragraph of Nabu-nadin-shumi's letter shows, scholars did much to support the king and to diffuse the load of decision making. The mechanism of requesting divine sanction for royal action by means of observing or inducing omens enabled the king to shift the burden of responsibility onto the shoulders of the gods, but it was, as we shall see, a negotiable process. The scholars had the means to persuade the gods to reverse their decisions if they were felt to be unfavorable to the king or land.

Esarhaddon's inscription commemorating the reconstruction of Ashur's temple depicts the king and his commission within a temporal continuum. Not only does the scholarly author take care to represent the architectural history of the building accurately, complete with revised positioning of previous acts of rebuilding within the quantified past; he also chooses an apposite propitious day in the present to mark the new enterprise. Further, he is able to imagine the process of building (already attested three times in the past and once in the present) iterated in the future. He has the king address posterity with these words: "I made monuments and inscriptions and I wrote on them the deeds I had done. For later kings my sons, I left them behind forever. May the kings my descendants, whose name Ashur calls for the lordship of the land and the people, see my monument and anoint it with oil, offer a libation, and return it to its place" (Ass A, VII.35–VIII.13; Borger 1956:6).

Just as Esarhaddon has respected the writings and deeds of his predecessors, future generations should venerate his. There is no sense here that time might come to an end; rather, Ashur and Assyria will endure in perpetuity and so will Esarhaddon's monuments, ensuring that his good name lives on for future generations. There is no hope for bodily immortality, but one's reputation may live forever in the collective memory. This is one of the many morals of the *Epic of Gilgamesh*: although Gilgamesh fails in his quest to attain eternal life, he is immortalized both through his monumental building works in the city of Uruk and through the enduring appeal of the *Epic* itself (George 1999).

Time's Arrow: Negotiating the Future

For kings to be able to represent their good and magnificent deeds to posterity they must earn the continuing support of the gods, by ensuring their actions did not run counter to the gods' desires. The gods could reveal their intentions for the world and the state in one of two ways. Specialist diviners could perform rituals to induce revealed omens in the entrails of sacrificed sheep and goats, as alluded to by Esarhaddon above. A manual of extispicy described the rituals to be performed (Starr 1983). The scholars formulated the king's question and laid it before the sheep or (later) wrote a report to the king after the outcome had been determined (Starr 1990).

Possible deviations from the normal configurations of the animals' innards and their ominous significance were systematically recorded and commented upon in a long treatise called *barutu* ("Extispicy") (Koch-Westenholz 2000). Here, immediately after Esarhaddon's death, the crown prince Ashurbanipal asks the sun-god Shamash whether his twin brother should be crowned king of Babylon in the spring *akitu* festival:

> I ask you Shamash great lord whether Shamash-shumu-ukin, son of Esarhaddon king of Assyria, should within this year seize the hand of the great lord Marduk in the Inner City (of Ashur) and lead Bel (= Marduk, to Babylon), whether it is pleasing to the great lord Marduk, whether it is acceptable to the great lord Marduk.
>
> Be present in this ram, place in it a firm and positive answer, favorable designs, favorable and propitious omens by the oracular command of your great divinity, and may I see them. May this query go to your great divinity, O Shamash great lord, and may an oracle be given as an answer. Nisannu (Month I), day 23, eponymate of Mari-larim (668 BCE). (Starr 1990:262)

It was also possible to read the gods' intentions by observing and deciphering the very configuration of the land and sky and even the bodies and behaviors of individuals: that is, in the world as Marduk created it. The omens relating to observable portentous phenomena on earth were collected together into four standard series, just as *enuma anu ellil* and *barutu* comprised the omens of the sky and the entrails of sacrificed animals. The terrestrial omen series was

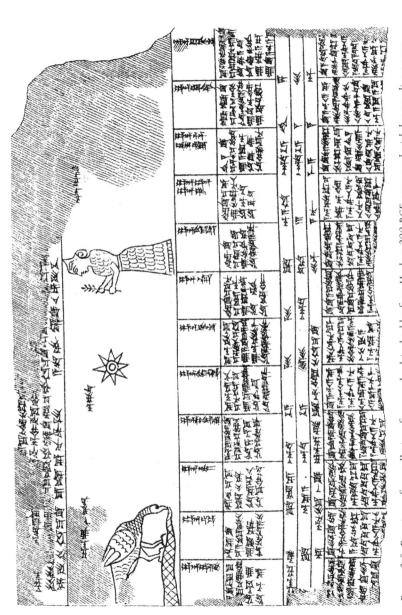

Figure 3.5 Drawings of constellations from a calendrical tablet from Uruk, c. 200 BCE, concerned with lunar eclipses near zodiacal constellations, showing the tail of the Serpent (Hydra), the Raven (Corvus), Attack (Mercury), and the Furrow (Virgo). From F. Thureau-Dangin, Tablettes d'Uruk à l'usage des prêtres du temple d'Anu au temps des Séleucides. Paris: Geuthner, 1922, no. 12.

called *shumma alu* ("If a City") (Freedman 1998), the teratological (birth) omen series *shumma izbu* ("If an Anomalous Birth") (Leichty 1969), the physiognomic omen series *alamdimmu* ("Physique") (Böck 2000) and the diagnostic omens *shumma ashipu* ("If an Incantation Priest") (Heessel 2000). As a 7th century catalogue of celestial and terrestrial omen series, the *Babylonian Diviner's Manual*, explains: "the signs on earth just as those in heaven give us signals. Sky and earth both produce portents: though appearing separately they are not separate: sky and earth are related (ll. 38–40; Oppenheimer 1974).

The catalog ends with complicated instructions on how to confirm or refute the validity of an omen by checking its date and time of day in a simple menology (Williams 2002).

Deviations in celestial motion from the ideal calendrical periodicities were considered particularly ominous as they indicated real-world slippage from ideal time. To this end, scholars kept observation records of lunar eclipses from the mid-8th century BCE, and later many other lunar, solar, and planetary phenomena, in so-called astronomical diaries, the latest of which is dated to 10 BCE (Sachs and Hunger 1988; Steele 2001). They soon discovered that lunar eclipses were possible (though not always visible) every six months, or sometimes every five, and that solar eclipses can occur 14–15 days before or after a lunar eclipse possibility. Such events were considered dangerous even when they were on schedule, but the omen series show that occurrences at unexpected times were an indication that the world was abnormally out of kilter with expectations. The ominous import of the timing of eclipses was covered in Tablet 19 of the celestial omen series *enuma anu ellil*; for instance: "If a lunar eclipse occurs on day 21 (of Tashritu = Month VII), and it sets during its eclipse: they will take the crowned king from his palace as a captive" (section III 13; Rochberg-Halton 1988:171).

Scholars would keep watch and report back to the king on the exact details of each celestial event and its ominous import, as exemplified here by the *tupshar enuma anu ellil* Nabu-ahhe-eriba's letter to Esarhaddon in Nisannu (Month I) 667 BCE: "Good health to the king, my lord. It is a dark day today, so I did not include a blessing. The eclipse moved from the east and settle over the entire west. Jupiter and Venus were present during the eclipse until it cleared. For the king my lord all is well; it is evil for Amurru. Tomorrow I shall send the king my lord a written report on this lunar eclipse" (Parpola 1993:75).

Because the eclipse pointed westward its influence would be felt in Amurru, to the west of Assyria, and once more the king and country were safe. If, however, the eclipse should unequivocally portend ill for Assyria itself, fate had to be averted. A substitute king was crowned and while the real king was ritually purified with lengthy and complicated ritual called *bit rimki* ("Bath House") (Laessoe 1955; Borger 1967). Here the Babylonian scholar Mar-Issar reports in Ululu (Month X) 671 BCE on the successfully averted evil of a lunar eclipse to Esarhaddon, who underwent *bit rimki* at least four times in his eleven-year reign: "The substitute king, who on the 14th sat on the throne in Nineveh and spent the night of the 15th in the royal palace, and on whom the eclipse took place, entered the city of Akkad safely on the night of the 20th and sat upon the throne. I made him recite the scribal recitations before the sun-god Shamash, he took all the celestial and terrestrial omens on himself, and ruled all the countries. The king, my lord, should know this" (Parpola 1993:351).

Sometimes, however, eclipses were not observed as predicted, but that did not necessarily mean that there was no danger. Either a positive sign of temporal normality was needed, or the full period of danger had to be endured, as Adad-shumu-usur here explains to Esarhaddon in 669 BCE: "As regards the substitute king about whom the king, my lord, wrote to me: 'how many days should he sit on the throne?', we waited for a solar eclipse, (but) the eclipse did not take place. Now, if the gods (i.e., sun and moon) are seen in opposition on the 15th day, he could go to his fate on the 16th. Or if it suits the king, my lord, better, he could (as well) sit the full 100 days" (Parpola 1993:220).

Omens, then, had expiration dates. But evil omens, it appears, did not necessarily have to be dodged by deflection onto another target. The gods could be persuaded to change their minds and to rewrite the great lapis lazuli Tablet of Destinies, on which they recorded their plans for the future of the supernatural and natural worlds. Its power is outlined in the *Epic of Creation* by evil chaos Tiamat as she gives it to her lover Qingu:

> Then she gave him the Tablet of Destinies and made him
>   clasp it to his breast.
> "Your utterance shall never be altered! Your word shall be
>   law!" (Tablet I, 157-58; Dalley 1989:238)

The idea is further elaborated in the *Epic of Anzu*, in which the eponymous anti-hero, a monstrous lion-eagle, steals the Tablet of Destinies from his godly master Ellil as he is relaxing in the bath:

> "I shall take the gods' Tablet of Destinies for myself
> And gather to myself all the responsibilities of the gods
> I shall possess the throne and be master of the rites!
> I shall direct every one of the Igigi-gods!"
> He plotted opposition in his heart
> And at the chamber's entrance from which he often gazed,
>   he waited for the start of day.
> While Ellil was bathing in the pure waters,
> Stripped and with his crown laid down on the throne,
> He gained the Tablet of Destinies for himself,
> Took away the Ellil-power. (Tablet I; Dalley 1989:207)

The gods are powerless without the Tablet, and Anzu is in complete control of the destiny of the world. Several gods refuse the challenge of combating Anzu, until the warrior-god Ninurta rises to the occasion. The two foes engage in a mighty cosmic battle. Anzu, with the Tablet of Destinies in his possession, is able to

Figure 3.6 The Anzu bird fought the heroic god Ninurta for possession of the Tablet of Destinies. This stone carving of the cosmic battle was erected in the temple of Ninurta at Kalhu, c. 875 BCE, and is now in the British Museum. Photograph by the author.

reverse the flow of time, temporally deflecting all attempts to kill him by returning the constituent parts of Ninurta's arrow to their original states:

> [Ninurta] set the shaft to the bow, drew it taut,
> Aimed the shaft at him from the bow's curve.
> But it did not go near Anzu: the shaft turned back.
> Anzu shouted at it, "You, shaft that came:
> Return to your reed thicket! Bow-frame: back to your copse!
> Bow-string: return to the ram's gut! Feathers: return to
>   the birds!"
> He was holding the gods' Tablet of Destinies in his hand,
> And they influenced the string of the bow: the arrows did
>   not come near his body.
> Deadly silence came over the battle, and conflict ceased.
> Weapons stopped and did not capture Anzu amid the mountains.
> (Tablet II, 59-69; Dalley 1989:214)

Eventually Ninurta is forced to find more cunning means to outwit his opponent and return the Tablet of Destinies to its rightful owner.

If the scholars could not persuade the gods to turn back the clock—in any case this was an abuse of the Tablet of Destinies—they could at least convince them to rewrite the future before it had happened. There were two methods for doing this. On the one hand there were *namburbu* incantations and rituals for removing evil, especially those portended by omens from the terrestrial series *shumma alu* and *shumma izbu*, which took the form of a trial, in front of three gods, of the supposed harbinger of evil (Maul 1994, 1999). Nabunadin-shumi delays such a ritual in his letter to Esarhaddon quoted above. There were also the *kalutu* rituals and laments, performed by the *kalu* lamentation priests during dangerous periods, in order to persuade the gods to let portended evil pass by. A legal record from Uruk in c.530 BCE, during the reign of the Persian king Cyrus, describes the public performance of a *kalutu* ritual in the nearby city of Larsa: "On Simanu (Month III), day 13, year 8 of Cyrus, king of Babylon, king of the lands, after sunset, the *kalus* of the E-babbar temple played the copper kettle-drum at the gate of the E-babbar and declared, 'Eclipse!', and all the inhabitants of Larsa saw with us the playing of the copper kettle-drum" (Beaulieu and Britton 1994:74, 17–22).

But it becomes clear from a related legal deposition, made by the chief *kalu* Shamash-tabni-usur of the Sin-leqi-unninni family, that the *kalus* had undertaken this performance without consulting their superiors at Uruk, and that the predicted eclipse did not in fact take place (Beaulieau and Britton 1994). The mismatch between prediction and actuality may have been one of the factors behind the reform of the intercalation cycle discussed above, instituted just a few years later in 527 BCE.

The 5th and 4th centuries saw a rapid growth in the scholars' power to predict ominous celestial events (Britton 1993). The corpus of astronomical diaries now amounted to several centuries of data, enabling even the longest planetary periodicities to be identified and described. The 5th-century invention of the zodiac as a celestial reference grid encouraged more accurate observations and predictions, but also had non-astronomical consequences. For instance, an elaborate calendrical scheme developed in the 5th century BCE that associated particular incantations and medical ingredients with each day of the ideal year. The so-called *Kalendertexte* scheme depended on a complex temporal relationship in which each of the twelve zodiacal signs is further subdivided into twelve "micro-signs." That in turn is intimately related to an idealised arithmetical scheme for representing lunar motion throughout the ideal year now called the Dodekatemoria (Brack-Bernsen and Steele, 2003). Even scholarly medical theory, then, was imbued with the idea of temporality.

The development of fully mathematical theoretical astronomy culminated in the late 4th century BCE. In Babylon at Marduk's temple Esangila the Mushezib family and others were closely associated with one style of predictive model, now called System A, while at the Resh temple in Uruk the Ekur-zakir and Sin-leqi-unninni families favored the scheme now known as System B (Neugebauer 1955). Both involved the tabulation of a mass of complex calculated data into ephemeredes, or predictions of the lunar, solar, and planetary positions for the coming year(s), computed according clearly laid out procedures. But still the rituals to avert the evil of an eclipse were performed. Predictable events were no less ominous; indeed it appears that their very predictability led to the performance of more elaborate apotropaic rituals than before, as one could now be sure that the expense would not be wasted (Brown and Linssen 1997). Lunar eclipse rituals from 3rd century Uruk involved massive public spectacle with drums, wailing, and the singing of Sumerian *balang* and *ershema* laments (Cohen 1988; Black 1991):

> On the day of the lunar eclipse they will bring the bronze *halhallatu* drum, the bronze *manzu* drum, and the bronze kettledrum from the storehouse. . . When the lunar eclipse begins, the *kalus* will put on linen garments. . . They raise lamentations, wailing, and mourning towards the moon in eclipse. . . .
>
> When the appearance of the eclipse is as one third of a disc, "The bull in its fold" is performed. They join in with "Mermer, a storm, who consumes life." The *ershema* is "Woe, he it is who has destroyed my *abzu*!" When the appearance of the eclipse is as two thirds of a disc, "The bull in its fold" and "Ah, woe is your heart" are performed. The *ershema* is "Woe, he it is who has destroyed my *abzu*!" They join in with "Mermer, a storm, who consumes life." . . .
>
> When the eclipse has cleared, they will leave the bronze kettledrum; they will leave the magic flour circle and the

kukkubbu-jar of [tamarisk] tears and cast the rest into the river.*

The scholarly tablets of the Sin-leqi-unninni family of *kalus* in 3rd-century Uruk include almost as many examples of apotropaic *kalutu* as they do mathematical predictive astronomy (Robson, forthcoming:chapter 9). Even Alexander the Great underwent the substitute king ritual in Babylon some time in the 320s BCE, as recounted in a rather garbled fashion by Plutarch in his *Life of Alexander*:

> On another occasion Alexander took off his clothes for exercise and played a game of ball. When it was time to dress again, the young men who had joined him in the game suddenly noticed that there was a man sitting silently on the throne and wearing Alexander's diadem and royal robes. When he was questioned, he could say nothing for a long while, but later he came to his senses and explained that he was a citizen of Messenia named Dionysus. He had been accused of some crime, brought to Babylonia from the coast, and kept for a long time in chains. Then the god Serapis had appeared to him, cast off his chains, and brought him to this place, where he had commanded him to put on the king's robe and diadem, take his seat on the throne, and hold his peace. When he had heard the man's story, Alexander had him put to death, as the diviners recommended. (73–74; trans. Scott-Kilvert 1973:330–331)

---

* BM 134701, lines 1'–4', 7'–10', 15'–16' (Brown and Linssen 1997:160–62). None of the three eclipse ritual tablets from Seleucid Uruk is dated, but Seleucid tablets of different *kalu* rituals from Uruk date from 289 and 230 BCE (AO 6472 and Ist O 174, Thureau-Dangin 1921:34–45) and 200, 176, and 165 BCE (van Dijk 1980:nos. 5, 6, 12). These latter tablets were excavated in the god Anu's temple, Resh.

Thus the coming of "scientific"—rather, quantitative—astronomy as a means of reliably predicting future celestial events did not annul their power as signs from the gods about their intentions for the terrestrial world.

The Temporal Order

How justifiable is it to examine this broad chronological and cross-generic sweep of evidence? I stated at the beginning that such an eclectic approach was typical of the scholars themselves. To demonstrate this, we shall look briefly at the contents of two scholarly libraries from the period under discussion. The temple library of Nabu, god of scholarship, in the Assyrian city of Kalhu was active over the 8th and 7th centuries BCE (Wiseman and Black 1996:4). Thirty of its three hundred tablets preserve colophons, some of which bear the names of an 8th-century family of royal *ashipus* while others bear the name of the scribe Nabu-zuqup-kena of the Gabbu-ilani-eresh family, who followed the royal court to Nineveh when it moved there in 705 BCE. Among its holdings were tablets from the standard terrestrial, celestial, teratological, diagnostic, and physiognomic omen series; the astronomical compendium MUL.APIN; hemerologies and menologies; apotropaic *namburbu* incantations and rituals; the *Epic of Creation* and the *Epic of Gilgamesh*; and royal inscriptions of the 9th to 7th centuries BCE.*

---

* In detail: 2 tablets of the astronomical compendium MUL.APIN ("Plough star"); 23 tablets of the celestial omen series *enuma anu ellil* ("When the gods Anu and Ellil"); 14 tablets of the terrestrial omen series *shumma alu* ("If a City"); 7 tablets of the teratological omen series *shumma izbu* ("If an Anomalous Birth"); 4 tablets of the menology *iqqur ipush* ("He Destroyed, He Built"); 6 tablets of hemerologies; 4 tablets of the sacrificial divination series *barutu* ("Extispicy") and 1 divinatory model of a sheep's lung; 3 tablets of the diagnostic omen series *shumma ashipu* ("If an Incantation Priest") and 1 catalogue of the series; 6 tablets of physiognomic omens; 10 tablets of apotropaic *namburbu* incantations; 1 tablet of the *Epic of Gilgamesh* and 2 tablets of the *Epic of Creation*; over 50 tablets of incantations and associated rituals; and an unknown number of royal inscriptions from the reigns of Shamshi-Adad V to Ashurbanipal (823–627 BCE) (Wiseman and Black 1996).

At the other end of the geographical, chronological, and contextual span of this chapter is the private library of the *ashipu* Iqisha of the Ekur-zakir family in Uruk. He left in his house nearly 250 scholarly compositions, household legal records, and school exercises. Thirty identifiable scholarly tablets, dated to the period 322–317 BCE, bear his name. They include tablets from almost all the standard series of omens, and commentaries on them; zodiacal-medical *Kalendertexte*; other astrology; apotropaic incantations and rituals.* Other tablets in the library not directly attributable to Iqisha himself include many more examples of the same types of composition, as well as lunar and planetary ephemeredes, hemerologies, and menologies, the *Epic of Gilgamesh*; *kalutu*, *namburbu*, and *bit rimki* incantations and rituals.†

In other words, the professional interests of both Iqisha and the Nabu temple scholars covered almost exactly the range of text-types discussed here. All that is missing are the equinoctial *akitu* rituals which, however, are known from 8th century Ashur and Nineveh and 3rd century Uruk as well as 1st millennium Babylon (Cohen 1993:420–53). Taking into account the fact that some compositions, such as MUL.APIN ("Plough Star") fell out of favor, while others, such as the *Kalendertexte* and the mathematical astronomical texts, were post-Assyrian inventions, the contents of the two libraries are

---

* In detail: 2 tablets of the calendrical scheme known as *Kalendertexte*, for Months IV and VIII; 3 tablets of quantitative astrology; 2 tablets with commentaries on the celestial omen series *enuma anu ellil* ("When the gods Anu and Ellil"); 4 tablets of the terrestrial omen series *shumma alu* ("If a City"); 2 tablets of commentaries on the teratological omen series *shumma izbu* ("If an Anomalous Birth"); 1 tablet of the diagnostic omen series *shumma ashipu* ("If an Incantation Priest"); 2 tablets of the sacrificial omen series *barutu* ("Extispicy") and commentaries; 9 tablets with series of incantations and associated rituals (Hunger 1976; von Weiher 1983–98). Findspot information in Hunger (1972) and von Weiher (1979).

† In detail: 2 lunar and planetary ephemeredes and 3 other astronomical works; 3 or 4 tablets of the *Epic of Gilgamesh*; 2 tablets of hemerologies; 3 tablets of the menology *iqqur ipush* ("He Destroyed, He Built"); 4 tablets of *namburbu* rituals to avert evil omens; 3 tablets of the series *bit rimki* ("Bath House") for the substitute king ritual; 1 tablet of the standard series associated with lamentation priests, *kalutu*; 1 tablet with a fragment of a royal inscription (Hunger 1976; von Weiher 1983–98). Findspot information in Hunger (1972) and von Weiher (1979).

remarkably similar. While some scribal circles, families, and individuals had particular interests and preferences, the scholars shared and developed a large body of knowledge and conceptions about time.

Issues of temporality permeated almost all aspects of scholarly endeavor, from medicine to divination, from literature to astronomy. The centrality of lunar cycle was affirmed and strengthened each new year with the performance of the *Epic of Creation*, in which creation, destruction, and renewal were prominent themes. The scholarly view of time as favorable or unfavorable, dangerous or safe dictated their patterns of professional activity and deeply influenced the timing of matters of state. Not only were royal events fixed according to the scholarly calendar but also great outlays of wealth and specialist personnel were expended on matters temporal. Enormous and elaborate public rituals, from *akitu* to *bit rimki*, *namburbu*, and *kalutu*, were each designed, in their different ways, to control and manage present and future time.

The constant intellectual battle to reconcile the ideal 360-day cycle of lunations with the solar and lunar years was a major driving force behind the development of observational astronomy in Assyria and Babylonia. Successive generations of scholars cooperated to produce a massive body of data and theory to describe and predict the motions of the heavenly bodies and thus unwittingly laid down the foundations on which the modern scientific concept of time is based.*

References

Beaulieu, P.-A. "The Impact of Month-lengths on the Neo-Babylonian Cultic Calendar." *Zeitschrift für Assyriologie* 83 (1993):66–87.

———. "The Descendants of Sin-leqi-unninni." In J. Marzahn and H. Neumann, eds., *Assyriologica et Semitica: Festschrift für Joachim Oelsner*. Alter Orient und Altes Testament 252. Münster: Ugarit-Verlag, 2000, 1–16.

---

* I am very grateful to Fran Reynolds, John Steele, and Niek Veldhuis for their efforts in making the this chapter more accurate and readable than it would otherwise have been.

Beaulieu, P.-A., and J. P. Britton. "Rituals for an Eclipse Possibility in the 8th year of Cyrus." *Journal of Cuneiform Studies* 46 (1994):73–86.

Bidmead, J. The akitu *Festival: Religious Continuity and Royal Legitimation in Mesopotamia.* Gorgias Dissertations. Near Eastern Series 2. Piscataway, NJ: Gorgias Press, 2002.

Black, J.A. "Eme-sal Cult Songs and Prayers." In P. Michalowski, P. Steinkeller, E. C. Stone, and R. L. Zettler, eds., *Velles Paraules: Ancient Near Eastern Studies in Honor of Miguel Civil on the Occasion of his Sixty-fifth Birthday.* Aula Orientalis 9. Barcelona: Editorial AUSA, 1991, 23–36.

Böck, B. *Die Babylonisch-Assyrisch Morphoskopie.* Archiv für Orientforschung, Beiheft 27. Horn: Berger, 2000.

Borger, R. *Die Inschriften Asarhaddons Königs von Assyrien.* Archiv für Orientforschung, Beiheft 9. Graz: E. Weidner, 1956.

———. "Das dritte 'Haus' der Serie Bit Rimki." *Journal of Cuneiform Studies* 21 (1967):1–17.

Bowen, A. C., and B. R. Goldstein. "Meton of Athens and Astronomy in the Late Fifth Century BC." In E. Leichty, M. J. Ellis, and P. Gerardi, eds., *A Scientific Humanist: Studies in Memory of Abraham Sachs.* Occasional Publications of the Samuel Noah Kramer Fund 9. Philadelphia: University of Pennsylvania Museum of Archaeology and Anthropology, 1988, 39–81.

Brack-Bernsen, L. "Predictions of Lunar Phenomena in Babylonian Astronomy." In J. M. Steele and A. Imhausen, eds., *Under One Sky: Astronomy and Mathemagics in the Ancient Near East* Alter Orient und Altes Testament 297. Münster: Ugarit-Verlag, 2002, 5–19.

Brack-Bernsen, L., and J. M. Steele. "Babylonian mathematics: In C. Burnett, J. P. Hogendijk, K. Plofker, and M. Yano eds., *Studies in the History of the Exact Sciences in Honour of David Pingree.* Leiden: Brill, 2003.

Britton, J. P. "Scientific Astronomy in Pre-Seleucid Babylon." In H. D. Galter, ed., *Die Rolle der Astronomie in den Kulturen Mesopotamiens.* Grazer Morgenländische Studien 3. Graz: rm-Druck- & Vergesellschaft mbH, 1993, 61–76.

———. "Treatments of Annual Phenomena in Cuneiform Sources." In J. M. Steele and A. Imhausen. eds., *Under One Sky: Astronomy and Mathematics in the Ancient Near East.* Alter Orient und Altes Testament 297. Münster: Ugarit-Verlag, 2002, 21–78.

Brown, D. R. *Mesopotamian Planetary Astronomy-Astrology.* Cuneiform Monographs 18. Groningen: Styx, 2000a.

———. "The Cuneiform Conception of Celestial Space and Time." *Cambridge Archaeological Journal* 10 (2000b):103–22.

Brown, D. R., J. Fermor, and C. B. F. Walker. "The Water Clock in Mesopotamia." *Archiv für Orientforschung* 46–47 (1999–2000):130–48.

Brown, D. R., and M. Linssen. "BM 134701 = 1965-10-14, 1 and the Hellenistic Period Eclipse Ritual from Uruk." *Revue d'Assyriologie et d'Archéologie Orientale* 91 (1997):147–66.

Cohen, M. E. *The Canonical Lamentations of Ancient Mesopotamia.* Bethesda, MD: CDL Press, 1988.

———. *The Cultic Calendars of the Ancient Near East.* Bethesda, MD: CDL Press, 1993.

Cole, S. W., and P. Machinist. *Letters from Priests to the Kings Esarhaddon and Assurbanipal.* State Archives of Assyria 13. Helsinki: Helsinki University Press, 1998.

Dalley, S. M. *Myths from Mesopotamia.* Oxford: Oxford University Press, 1989.

Englund, R. K. "Administrative Timekeeping in Ancient Mesopotamia." *Journal of the Economic and Social History of the Orient* 31 (1998):121–85.

———. "Hard Work—Where Will It Get You? Labor Management in Ur III Mesopotamia" *Journal of Near Eastern Studies* 50 (1991):255–80.

Fermor, J., and J. M. Steele. "The Design of Babylonian Waterclocks: Astronomical and Experimental Evidence." *Centaurus* 42 (2000):210–22.

Finkel, I. L., and J. E. Reade. "Lots of Eponyms." *Iraq* 57 (1995): 167–72.

Freedman, S. M. *If a City is Set on a Height* I. Occasional Publications of the Samuel Noah Kramer Fund 17. Philadelphia, PA: University of Pennsylvania Museum of Archaeology and Anthropology, Babylonian Section, 1998.

Geller, M. "The Last Wedge." *Zeitschrift für Assyriologie* 87 (1997):43–96.

George, A. R. *The Epic of Gilgamesh: A New Translation*. London: Allen Lane, 1999.

Grayson, A. K. "Königslisten und Chroniken." *Reallexikon der Assyriologie* 6 (1980):86–135.

———. *Assyrian Rulers of the Third and Second Millennia BC (to 1115 BC)*. Royal Inscriptions of Mesopotamia. Assyrian Periods 1. Toronto: University of Toronto Press, 1987.

Harper, P. O., E. Klengel-Brandt, J. Aruz, and K. Benzel. *Assyrian Origins: Discoveries at Ashur on the Tigris: Antiquities in the Vorderasiatisches Museum, Berlin*. New York, Metropolitan Museum of Art: 1995.

Heessel, N. P. *Babylonisch-Assyrische Diagnostik*. Alte Orient, Altes Testament 43. Münster: Ugarit-Verlag, 2000.

Horowitz, W. *Mesopotamian Cosmic Geography*. Mesopotamian Civilizations 8. Winona Lake, IN: Eisenbrauns, 1998.

Hunger, H. 1972. "Die Tontafeln der XXVII. Kampagne." In J. Schmidt, ed., *XXVI. und XXVII. vorläufige Bericht über die von dem Deutschen Archäologischen Institut und der Deutsche Orient-Gesellschaft aus Mitteln der Deutschen Forschungsgemeinschaft unternommen Ausgrabungen in Uruk-Warka, 1968 und 1969.* Berlin: Mann, 1972, 79–87.

———. *Spätbabylonische Texte aus Uruk* I. Ausgrabungen der Deutschen Forschungsgemeinschaft in Uruk-Warka. Endberichte 9. Berlin: Mann, 1976.

———. *Astrological Reports to Assyrian Kings.* State Archives of Assyria 8. Helsinki: Helsinki University Press, 1992.

———. "Zeitmessung." In J. Høyrup and P. Damerow, eds., *Changing Views on Ancient Near Eastern Mathematics* Berliner Beiträger zum Vorderen Orient 19. Berlin: Riemer, 2001, 311–16.

Hunger, H., and D. Pingree. *MUL.APIN. An Astronomical Compendium in Cuneiform.* Archiv für Orientforschung 24. Horn: Berger, 1989.

———. *Astral Sciences in Mesopotamia.* Handbuch der Orientalistik 44. Leiden: Brill, 1999.

Koch-Westenholz, U. *Babylonian Liver Omens: The Chapters Manzazu, Padanu and Pan Takalti of the Babylonian Extispicy Series Mainly from Assurbanipal's Library.* Carsten Niebuhr Institute Publications 25. Copenhagen: Museum Tusculanum Press, 2000.

Labat, R. *Hémérologies et menologies d'Assur.* Paris: Adrien-Maisonneuve, 1939.

———. "Un Almanach Babylonien (V 48–49)." *Revue d'Assyriologie* 38 (1941):13–40.

———. *Un Calendrier Babylonien des Travaux des Signes et des Mois (series iqqur ipush).* Paris: Champion, 1965.

Laessoe, J. *Studies on the Assyrian Ritual and Series Bit Rimki.* Copenhagen: Munksgaard, 1955.

Landsberger, B. *Der Kultische Kalender der Babylonier und Assyrer.* Leipzig: Hinrichs, 1915.

Leichty, E. *The Omen Series Shumma Izbu.* Texts From Cuneiform Sources 4. Locust Valley, NY: Augustin, 1969.

———. "The Origins of Scholarship." In H. D. Galter, ed., *Die Rolle der Astronomie in den Kulturen Mesopotamiens.* Grazer Morgenländische Studien 3. Graz: rm-Druck- & Vergesellschaft mbH, 1993, 21–29.

Livingstone, A. "The Case of the Hemerologies: Official Cult, Learned Formulations, and Popular Practice." In E. Matsushima, ed., *Official Cult and Popular Religion in the Ancient Near East.* Heidelberg: Universitätsverlag C. Winter, 1993, 97–113.

———. "The Magic of Time." In T. Abusch and K. van der Toorn, eds., *Mesopotamian Magic: Textual, Historical, and Interpretative Perspectives.* Ancient Magic and Divination 1. Groningen: Styx, 1999, 131–37.

Maul, S. M. *Zukunftsbewältigung: eine Untersuchung altorientalischen Denkens anhand der babylonisch-assyrischen Löserituale (Namburbi).* Bahdader Mitteilungen, Beiheft 18. Mainz: von Zabern, 1994.

———. "How Babylonians Protected Themselves Against Calamities Announced by Omens." In T. Abusch and K. van der Toorn, eds., *Mesopotamian Magic: Textual, Historical, and Interpretative Perspectives.* Ancient Magic and Divination 1. Groningen: Styx, 1999, 123–29.

Michalowski, P. "Commemoration, Writing, and Genre in Ancient Mesopotamia." In C. S. Kraus, ed., *The Limits of Historiography: Genre and Narrative in Ancient Historical Texts.* Leiden: Brill, 1999, 69–90.

Millard, A. R. *The Eponyms of the Assyrian Empire 910–612 BC*. State Archives of Assyria Studies 2. Helsinki: Neo-Assyrian Text Corpus Project, 1994.

Neugebauer, O. *Astronomical Cuneiform Texts: Babylonian Ephemeredes of the Seleucid Period for the Motion of the Sun, the Moon, and the Planets*. London: Princeton Institute for Advanced Study, 1955.

Oppenheim, A. L. "A Babylonian Diviner's Manual." *Journal of Near Eastern Studies* 33 (1974):197–220.

Parpola, S. "The Forlorn Scholar." In F. Rochberg-Halton, ed., *Language, Literature, and History: Philological and Historical Studies Presented to Erica Reiner*. American Oriental Series 67. New Haven, CT: American Oriental Society, 1961–87, 257–78.

———. *Letters from Assyrian and Babylonian Scholars*. State Archives of Assyria 10. Helsinki: Helsinki University Press, 1993.

Pedersén, O. *Archives and Libraries in the Ancient Near East, 1500–300 BC*. Bethesda, MD: CDL Press, 1998.

Robbins, E. "Tabular Sacrifice Records and the Cultic Calendar of Neo-Babylonian Uruk." *Journal of Cuneiform Studies* 48 (1996):61–87.

Robson, E. "Technology in Society: Three Textual Case Studies from Late Bronze Age Mesopotamia." In A.J. Shortland, ed., *The Social Context of Technological Change: Egypt and the Near East 1650–1150 BC*. Oxford: Oxbow, 2001, 39–57.

———. forthcoming. *Mathematics in Ancient Iraq: a Social History*. Princeton, NJ: Princeton University Press.

Rochberg-Halton, F. *Aspects of Babylonian Celestial Divination: the Lunar Eclipse Tables of Enuma Anu Enlil*. Archiv für Orientforschung, Beiheft 22. Horn: Berger, 1988.

Rochberg, F. "The Cultural Locus of Astronomy in Late Babylonia." In H. D. Galter, ed., *Die Rolle der Astronomie in den Kulturen Mesopotamiens.* Grazer Morgenländische Studien 3. Graz: rm-Druck- & Vergesellschaft mbH, 1993, 31–45.

———. "Scribes and Scholars: the *tupshar Enuma Anu Enlil.*" In J. Marzahn and H. Neumann, eds., *Assyriologica et Semitica: Festschrift für Joachim Oelsner.* Alter Orient und Altes Testament 252. Münster: Ugarit-Verlag, 2000, 359–76.

Sachs, A. J. "The Latest Datable Cuneiform Texts." In B. L. Eichler, ed., *Kramer Anniversary Volume: Cuneiform Studies in Honor of Samuel Noah Kramer.* Alter Orient und Altes Testament 25. Kevelaer: Butzon & Bercker, 1976, 379–98.

Sachs, A. J., and H. Hunger. *Astronomical Diaries and Related Texts from Babylonia I–III.* Vienna: Österreichische Akademie der Wissenschaften, 1998.

Scott-Kilvert, I. *The Age of Alexander: Nine Greek Lives by Plutarch.* Harmondsworth: Penguin, 1973.

Snow, C. P. *The Two Cultures and the Scientific Revolution.* Cambridge: Cambridge University Press, 1959.

Sommer, B. D. "The Babylonian Akitu festival: Rectifying the King or Renewing the Cosmos?" *Journal of the Ancient Near Eastern Society* 27 (2000):81–95.

Starr, I. *The Rituals of the Diviner.* Malibu, CA: Undena, 1983.

———. *Queries to the Sungod: Divination and Politics in Sargonid Assyria.* State Archives of Assyria 4. Helsinki: Helsinki University Press, 1990.

Steele, J. M. "The Latest Dated Astronomical Observation from Babylon." In A. Millard, ed., *Archaeological Sciences '97.* BAR International Series 939. Oxford: Archaeopress, 2001, 208–11.

Streck, M. *Assurbanipal und die letzten assyrischen Könige bis zum Untergange Ninivehs.* Vorderasiatische Bibliothek 7. Leipzig: Hinrichs, 1916.

Thureau-Danin, F. *Rituels accadiens.* Paris: Leroux, 1921.

van Dijk, J., and W. Mayer. *Texte aus dem Resh-Heiligtum in Uruk.* Baghdader Mitteilungen, Beiheft 2. Berlin: Mann, 1980.

von Weiher, E. "Die Tontafelfunde der XXIX. und XXX. Kampagne." In J. Schmidt, ed., *XXIX. und XXX. vorläufige Bericht über die von dem Deutschen Archäologischen Institut aus Mitteln der Deutschen Forschungsgemeinschaft unternommen Ausgrabungen in Uruk-Warka, 1970/71 und 1971/72.* Berlin: Mann, 1979, 95–111.

———. *Spätbabylonische Texte aus Uruk II–V.* Ausgrabungen der Deutschen Forschungsgemeinschaft in Uruk-Warka. Endberichte 10–13. Berlin: Mann, 1983–98.

Williams, C. "Signs from the Sky, Signs from the Earth: the Diviner's Manual Revisited." In J. M. Steele and A. Imhausen, eds., *Under One Sky: Astronomy and Mathematics in the Ancient Near East.* Alter Orient und Altes Testament 297. Münster: Ugarit-Verlag, 2002, 473–85.

Wiseman, D. J., and J. A. Black. *Literary Texts from the Temple of Nabu.* Cuneiform Texts from Nimrud 4. London: British School of Archaeology in Iraq, 1996.

CONCEPTS OF TIME IN CLASSICAL INDIA

Ludo Rocher

The belief that the present world and its inhabitants exist in an age of privation and distress is not unique to India, nor is the expectation that this situation is only a temporary one, that it degenerated from earlier better ages, and that better ages, including the ideal age, will return (Meyer 1922; Eliade 1959). Nowhere, however, is this belief as omnipresent and as elaborately developed as in India. It is still referred to in traditional Indian calendars (*pancāngas*) (Sewell and Dikshit 1896:40–41). In India, successive, endlessly successive, smaller and larger world ages, some of them separated by world destructions and world creations, have been worked out into "a system, which is as typically Indian, as it is unparalleled with other peoples" (Gonda 1948:41).

Inevitably, Indian conceptions of time attracted the attention of foreign visitors. Even though, as a Muslim, the 11th century polymath and traveler to India, al-Bîrûnî, was critical of Hindu and Buddhist "silly tales" and of statements by some Indian astronomers, he devoted 12 successive chapters of his *Tarikh al-Hind* to a detailed analysis of the Indian conceptions of time (al-Biruni 1964:327–88;

also on Rashîd al-Dîn, Jahn 1957). Seven centuries later, in the Preface to the *Code of Gentoo Laws*, a digest of Hindu law commissioned by Governor-General Warren Hastings and translated into English by Nathaniel Brassey Halhed (1776). Halhed expressed his amazement about the Hindu world ages: "Computation is lost, and conjecture overwhelmed in the attempt to adjust such astonishing spaces of time to our own confined notions of the world's epoch: to such antiquity the Mosaic Creation is but as yesterday; and to such ages the life of Methuselah is no more than a span!" (R. Rocher 1983; Marshall 1970:158–159). The first president of the Asiatic Society in Calcutta (founded in 1784), Sir William Jones, contributed an article "On the Chronology of the Hindus" to the Society's journal, the *Asiatick Researches* (1788), in which he "venture[d] to start a question, 'whether it is not in fact the same as our own, but embellished and obscured by the fancy of their poets and the riddles of their astronomers'" (Marshall 1970:262). To be sure, James Mill was not impressed by the Orientalists in Calcutta who considered Hindu conceptions of time "entitled to a very serious and profound investigation." For him, Indian conceptions of time, "[t]he offspring of a wild and ungoverned imagination, . . . mark the state of a rude and credulous people, whom the marvelous delights; who cannot estimate the use of a record of past events; and whose imagination the real occurrences of life are too familiar to engage" (Mill 1840:163, 166).

Indian Systems of Cyclical Time

The Jaina, Buddhist, and, especially, Hindu systems of world ages and cyclical time have been described repeatedly. In this comparative volume on the concepts of time in different ancient civilizations I will again briefly describe the Indian systems, but then concentrate on the disputed question: is the Indian system of cyclical time indigenous to the subcontinent, or did the Indians borrow it from another ancient civilization?

The basic idea in Hindu cyclical time is that four world ages, called *yugas*, succeed each other with no interruption (Jacobi 1908; Abegg 1918; Eliade 1957; Kane 1958:686–718; Brown 1966:68–87; Reimann 1988). Throughout these four periods everything goes diminuendo—time itself, people's life spans, their intelligence, and their morals and standards of behavior (*dharma*). At the end of the fourth and worst period Vishnu descends on earth in the form his tenth *avatàra*, Kalki(n), and reinstates the new "golden age."

Differently from, for instance, Hesiod's world ages which derive their names from gradually less-precious metals, the names of the Indian *yugas* correspond to those of diminishing throws of dice, a game that was popular in ancient India (Lüders 1907). *Krita* is the throw that is "made, well made, perfect"; Vittore Pisani (1943) connected the term *krita* with the numeral 4. The first period is also called *satya-yuga*, the "truth-age," the age in which everything is as it ought to be. *Tretà* is clearly related to the number 3 and *dvàpara* to the number 2; the etymology of *kali* is uncertain: the connection of *kali* with Sanskrit *kàla* ("time") or *kàla* ("black"), or with the goddess Kâlî is based on Indian popular etymology (Abegg 1928:20–21).

Differently also from other civilizations which share the concept of successive world ages, Indians have quantified the four *yugas*, in the diminishing ratio of 4 : 3 : 2 : 1. The duration of the *yugas* is based on the sequence 4,000 : 3,000 : 2,000 : 1,000, to each of which the texts usually add dawns (*sandhyà*) and twilights (sandhyànsha) equal to one-tenth of the *yuga*, which leads to *yugas* of 4,800, 3,600, 2,400, and 1,200 years. The ratio 4 : 3 : 2 : 1 is maintained throughout: the human lifespan diminishes from 400 years in the *kritayuga* to 100 years in the *kaliyuga*; *dharma* (often depicted as a cow) stands on four legs in the *kritayuga*, looses one leg in each of the next two, and stands on only one leg in the dismal *kaliyuga*.

Most texts then introduce a different concept. The duration of the *yugas* must be understood not in terms of human years, but in terms of divine years, a human year corresponding to one divine day an old concept going back to the *Taittirîya Brâhmana* (3.9.22.1).

Hence all figures mentioned so far are multiplied by 360: the *kritayuga* lasts 1,728,000 years, the *tretàyuga* 1,296,000 years, the *dvàparayuga* 864,000 years, the *kaliyuga* 432,000 years, and the total of the four *yugas*—the *caturyuga* or *mahàyuga*—lasts 4,320,000 years.

Immediately after the last *kaliyuga* of the *caturyuga*, the first dawn of a new *caturyuga* sets in, and this process is repeated one thousand times, without interruption. This period of one thousand *caturyugas*, i.e., 4,320,000,000 human years, is given the name of either *kalpa* or "day of Brahmà."* A "day of Brahmà" is naturally followed by a "night of Brahmà," of the same duration, so that one nychthemeron of Brahmà comprises 8,640,000,000 years. Differently from the shorter time periods (*yugas* and *caturyugas*), which follow each other without interruption, the day of Brahmà is followed by a world destruction (*pralaya*), and the night of Brahmà is followed by a world creation.

Brahmà does not live just nychthemeron. He lives a full life, and, in ancient India, according to the *Rigveda* (1.89.9, 1.64.14., 2.33.2), the ideal life span was considered to be one hundred years. The life of Brahmà (also called *mahàkalpa*), therefore, corresponds to 8,640,000,000 · 360 · 100 = 311,040,000,000,000 human years.

Finally—and here exactitude gives way to speculation—some texts go on to say that the present Brahmà has been preceded by and will be followed by numerous other Brahmàs (Fleet 1911:483, n.1). Or, they say that one life of Brahmà is equal to one day, or to just one eyewink of Vishnu (Burgess and Whitney 1860: 155). Irrespective of the way in which it is justified, the point is that cyclical time in Hinduism is eternal, without beginning or end (Jones 1788, in Marshall 1970:265).

To complete the picture of cyclical time in Hinduism, we must note that, along with the *yugas*, a second system of cycles evolves. Within each *kalpa*, i.e., within a period of 1,000 *caturyugas*,

---

* Even though Sanskrit words are usually cited in the stem form, I use the masculine nominative form brahmà, to distinguish the god Brahmà (stem brahmán) from the neuter abstract principle bráhman (nominative brahma).

there are 14 *manvantaras* "intervals of Manu." Each *manvantara* has it own Manu patriarch, its own gods, and its own sages (*rishi*). Since a *kalpa* of 1,000 *caturyugas* is not divisible by 14, some texts, including the *Manusmriti* and Brahmagupta (Fleet 1911:486), say that a *manvantara* corresponds to 71 *caturyugas*, a total of 994 *caturyugas*, which leaves 6 *caturyugas* unaccounted for (*Màrkandeya puràna* 46.34). Some texts leave it at that (Kane 1946:891). According to other texts, each *manvantara* comprises 72 *caturyugas*, 1,008 *caturyugas* in all, i.e., an excess of 8 *caturyugas* (Shukla 1976:197). Other texts again work with 71 *caturyugas*, and divide the 6 remaining *caturyugas* into 15 juncture periods (*sandhi*) of 0.4 *caturyugas* each, which they insert before the first and after all 14 *manvantaras*, (14 *manvantaras* · 71) + (0.4 *manvantaras* · 15) = 1,000 *caturyugas*, a system adopted by the *Sûryasiddhânta* (1.18–19) (Burgess and Whitney 1860:154; Fleet 1911:486).

These details demonstrate how the *manvantara* system, the origin of which is unknown, was gradually and rather uncomfortably forced to fit within the *yuga/kalpa* system: Pusalker (1955) considers the insertion of 71 *manvantaras* into a *kalpa* "purely hypothetical and a later elaboration" (lvi).

Hindu texts also speculate on the beginning of the present *kaliyuga*, all speculations being connected with events in the *Mahâbhârata*. The Indian astronomers fixed the beginning of the *kaliyuga* at midnight between 17 and 18 February 3101 B.C.E. (Pingree 1963:239). The Hindus now live in the 457th (of 1,000) *caturyuga* and the seventh (of 14) *manvantara* of the 18,001st (of 36,000) *kalpa*/day of Brahmâ. The present day of Brahmâ is called *Varâhakalpa*; the present Manu is Manu Vaivasvata.

Differently from Hinduism, Jainism does accept both descending and ascending time periods (Glasenapp 1964:262–310; Jaini 1979:30–32; Reimann 1988:114–16). These periods follow one another without any interruption. For the Jainas the world exists permanently and eternally, without any intervening world destruction. Time is viewed as a turning wheel (*cakra*) whose 12 spokes constantly revolve downward and upward. The 6 parts of the *avasarpinî* ("descending") half of the cycle are: (1) the *sushamâ-sushamâ* ("good-good"), (2) *sushamâ* ("good"), (3) *sushamâ-dushshamâ* ("good-bad"), (4) *dushshamâ-sushamâ* ("bad-good"), (5) *dushshamâ* ("bad"), and *dushshamâ-dushshamâ* ("bad-bad") periods. After the end of the *avasarpinî*, the 6 periods follow one another again, in reverse order, in the *utsarpinî* ("upward") half of the cycle.

Like Hinduism, Jainism assigns numbers, though less specific numbers, of years to the duration of each time period. They are expressed neither in human or divine years, but are far vaster and less clearly defined: *kotikotis* of *sàgaropamas*. A *koti* (modern "crore") corresponds to 10,000,000. One *sàgaropama* itself equals ten *kotikotis* of *palyopamas*, one *palyopama* being the time needed to empty a container one *yojana* [i.e., 4 miles or more!] in diameter and one *yojana* high, filled with tender hairs, if one removes one hair every 100 years (Glasenapp 1964:155). Even as in Hinduism, in Jainism the duration of the 4 best periods is in the ratio of 4 : 3 : 2 : 1 : four *kotikotis* of *sàgaropamas,* three, etc. Except that, from the fourth best period, the Jainas subtract 42,000 years that are equally divided into 21,000 years assigned to the fifth and sixth periods. We now live in the fifth period of the *avasarpinî*, which started three years after the death of Mahâvîra (Stevenson 1915:275).

It is obvious that the Jainas, following the typically Indian tendency of enlarging existing numeral systems, made an effort to adopt the Hindu system of cyclical time within their ever-revolving wheel of time, a concept that goes back to the Vedas (*Rigveda* 1.164.14) (Brown 1968:213).

Buddhist cyclical time operates with numbers which are as speculative as those of Jainism (LaVallée-Poussin 1908; Bareau 1975; Kloetzli 1983). Even as Hinduism, Buddhism operates with *kalpas*, usually called *mahàkalpas*, which follow one another endlessly. Even as the *yugas* in Hinduism, the Buddhist *kalpas* are 4 in number, in this order: (1) a *kalpa* of renovation (*vivarta*), (2) a *kalpa* during which the world remains renovated (*vivartàvasthàyin*), (3) a *kalpa* of destruction (*sanvarta*), and (4) a *kalpa* in which the world remains destroyed (*sanvartàvasthàyin*). Differently from Hinduism and from Jainism, the duration of the *mahàkalpas* is *asankheyya* (Pali; Sanskrit *asankhyeya*) ("incalculable") literally "not to be expressed in numbers." One favorite description of *asankheyya* is as follows: "It is as if there were a mountain consisting of a great rock, a league in length, a league in width, a league in height, without break, cleft, or hollow, and every hundred years a man were to come and rub it once with a silken garment; that mountain consisting of a great rock would more quickly wear away and come to an end than a world-cycle" (Warren 1896:315, n. 1).

The fact that the incalculable *mahàkalpas* are subdivided into 20 *antarakalpas* ("intermediate *kalpas*") is unimportant for our present purpose. What is important is that, within the twentieth and last *antarakalpa* of the *mahàkalpa* in which the world remains renovated, the Buddhists insert 4 brief periods of increase and 4 equally brief periods of decrease. And these periods are, once again, designated with the names of the Hindu *yugas*: *kali*, *dvàpara*, *tretà*, and *krita* in an ascending period, and *krita*, *tretà*, *dvàpara*, and *kali* in a descending sequence.

In other words, even as the Jainas, the Buddhists worked out a system of cyclical time of their own. Yet, they, too, felt obliged to reserve a niche to incorporate the Hindu yuga system in it.

The Origin of the Hindu *Yuga/Kalpa* System

The foregoing description of the three systems of cyclical time confirms Thomas Trautmann's evaluation that "[n]ames and numbers differ among the different religions, but it is plain that we are dealing with variants of a single patron, a unitary Indian intellectual culture of time." As far as Jainism and Buddhism are concerned, he underscores the "gross structural similarities with the Hindu system," and views their systems of time as "deliberate distortions and redefinitions of Hindu schemes that read like parodies" (Trautmann 1995:171). Louis de La Vallée-Poussin notes that the fanciful ideas of cyclical time "do not appear to be essential to Buddhism, whether looked upon as a religion or as a philosophy. Nor are they of mythological moment, being rather matter of 'secular knowledge,' or, as the Buddhists would say, *Lokàyika*" (1908:188). The Jainas, too, are less concerned with the global scheme of the endlessly rotating wheel of time; their only concern is "the current *avasarpinî* and that small area where human life is enacted" (Dundas 1991:18). When we look for the origin of the concept of cyclical time in India, it is, therefore, the origin of cyclical in Hinduism that is of primary importance.

The Hindu system of *yugas* and *kalpas*, as described, is absent from the oldest, Vedic literature, but it is omnipresent in later texts: the *Manusmriti*, the *Mahàbhàrata* (Bühler 1886:lxxxiii–xc), the *Puràṇas*, the treatises of most schools of Hindu philosophy, inscriptions, and the works of the Indian astronomers. Hence the alternative: either the system developed within India under the impulse of the composers of one or more of the later sources, or one of the later sources borrowed the system from outside India. It is my purpose to propose a third, different origin of the *yuga/kalpa* system of cyclical time.

The theory that cyclical time developed inside India in the post-Vedic period is most prominent in the writings of scholars of Indian philosophy (Schayer 1938; Mandal 1968). Paul Deussen (1920), a scholar and admirer of Shankara's *advaita* Vedànta philosophy, tried to prove that the theory of endless world creations and world destructions was elaborated within Vedànta, as early as Gaudapàda and Shankara, perhaps even in Bàdaràyana's *Vedântasûtras*. Vedànta needed to create that concept to reconcile the beginningless course of *sansàra*, forever determined by actions in previous existences, with the Upanishadic term *agre* ("in the beginning"). To harmonize the two contradictory views, Vedànta interpreted *agre* in the Upanishads as referring to the beginning of successive new world creations. According to Richard Garbe (1895), who wrote the first comprehensive study of Sànkhya philosophy, India's fascination with high numbers, which manifests itself in the teachings of all disciplines, must be traced back to the Sànkhya system—the term "Sànkhya" derives from *sankhyà* ("number")— and the doctrine of world ages originated within Sànkhya philosophy. Garbe maintained that the concept of world ages was first taken over from Sànkhya by Buddhism and Jainism, and only later, after the "brahmanization" of Sànkhya, by brahmanical literature (56, 222). In a review of *Die Sànkhya Philosophie*, Jacobi (1895) refuted Garbe's theses: the numbers in Sânkhya are "äusserst bescheiden" as compared to those of Jainism and Buddhism, and Garbe failed to prove that evolution and reabsorption of the world are necessary consequences of Sânkhya philosophy" (209–10).

The theory that Indian cyclical time is not of Indian but of foreign origin results from the belief that the *yuga*/*kalpa* system was created by Indian astronomers who borrowed it from foreigners, especially the Babylonians. Nearly a century ago F. Röck (1910) argued that all the numbers used in Hindu cyclical time, from the *caturyuga* down to the individual *yugas*, both with and without dawns and twilights, were known in Babylonia around 2400 BCE; the correspondences cannot be accidental, they result from "eine allgemeine Verbreitung babylonischer Kultur."

There is no doubt that the Indian astronomers made important contributions to the concept of time and world ages, nor is there any doubt that, in their computations, they borrowed heavily from their Babylonian—and other—counterparts (Pingree 1978a:3; 1978b). Entire passages in the works of the Indian astronomers became understandable only after comparing them with Babylonian sources (Neugebauer 1957:172). Yet, such borrowing does not mean that concepts of cyclical time and world ages separated by destruction and recreation may not have existed in India outside the circle of the astronomers, and at a time that antedates their works (Fleet 1911:484).

The principal point of comparison is the *kalpa* of 4,320,000,000 years. As David Pingree pointed out, "[t]his is a Babylonian number: sexagesimally it would be written 2,0,0,0. It is the span of time given to the Babylonian kingdom before the Flood in the histories of Berossos and Abydenus" (1963:238; see also van der Waerden 1952:150, 1977/78:363). According to Pingree, it is most likely that the number became known in India at the time of the Achaemenid occupation of the northwest: the term *kalpa* does appear in Ashoka's inscriptions (Hultzsch 1969:31, 33) and in the *Dîghanikâya* (Carpenter 1911:51, 111). "This *kalpa* of ultimately Babylonian origin was combined by the Indian astronomers of the late 4th and 5th century with the Greek epicyclic theory" (Pingree 1963:239). With the *kalpa* as the starting point, the smaller periods are described as later developments: "Each *kalpa* is divided into 1,000 equal parts called *mahàyugas* which are 4,320.000 years apiece, and each *mahàyuga* contains four smaller *yugas* which are in the ratio to each other of 4:3, 3:2, and 2:1. The last *yuga*, then, the *kaliyuga* is 1/10 *mahàyuga*, or 432,000 years" (Pingree 1963:238).

I wish to argue that the concept of cyclical time and world ages may have grown in India itself, not from the larger *kalpa* down to the smaller units, but from the smaller units up to the *kalpa* (Burgess and Whitney 1860:155), the length of which happened to coincide with the Babylonian number 4,320,000,000. In fact, the centerpiece of the entire system is the age in which we now live, i.e., the shortest period, the *kaliyuga*. No period has been described in as great detail in the texts as the *kaliyuga*, not so much because it was better known than any other (Sharma 1982; Yadava 1979), but because it was "the most important part in the whole scheme, since . . . the beginning of it is the pivot of the whole system" (Fleet 1911:480).

First, we may not forget that man, living in the jungles of ancient India, "[felt] himself indissolubly connected with the Cosmos and the cosmic rhythms" (Eliade 1959:vii). He noticed cycles in his own life and expanded them into cosmic cycles. Hence, the passage from the *Manusmriti* (1.64–74), which is often quoted for its description of cyclical time, proceeds uninterruptedly from the smallest unit of time, the *nimesha* ("eyeblink"), to the *kalpa*. It defines the length of each larger unit strictly in terms of the length of the immediately shorter one: 18 *nimeshas* equal 1 *kàsthà*; 30 *kàsthàs* equal 1 *kalà*; 30 *kalàs* equal 1 *muhûrta* ; 30 *muhûrtas* equal 1 nychthemeron; 1 month equals 1 day of the manes; 1 year equals one day of the gods; 4,800 divine years equal 1 *kritayuga* ; the other three *yugas* are each 1,100 years shorter than the preceding one; 12,000 divine years equal one age of the gods; 1,000 ages of the gods equal 1 one day of Brahmà, which is followed by a night of Brahmà of equal length, and a new creation (for a similar progression in other texts see Kirfel 1967:333–39; Glasenapp 1964:154–55).

Second, we know, and historians of mathematics have not failed to notice, that, from early onward, Indians were able to conceive unusually high numbers (Menninger 1957:147; Thibaut 1899:70; Clark 1937:343–344). Even in Vedic times, in counting the bricks that are required to erect the altar for a sacrifice (Weber 1861:134), the *Vàjasaneyisanhità* and other texts contain names for powers of ten up to the 16th (Macdonell and Keith 1958:342–343; Wackernagel 1930:375–78); Buddhism and Jainism went even farther than Hinduism. Even as Macdonell and Keith, Bibhutibhusan Datta and Avadhesh N. Singh stress that "from the very earliest known times, ten has formed the basis of enumeration in India" (1962:9; see also Fleet 1911:486, n. 1).

Third, as far as the number 432,000 is concerned, it, too, appears in Vedic literature. To be sure, in the Vedic texts the number 432,000 refers not to world ages but to the number of syllables in the *Rigveda*. The *Rigveda* is said to consist of 12,000 verses called *brihatî* , at 36 syllables each, or 432,000 syllables. Similarly, the *Yajurveda* is said to consist of 8,000 *brihatîs* · 36 = 288,000 syllables, and the *Sàmaveda* is said to comprise 4,000 *brihatîs* · 36 = 144,000 syllables. That means that the number of syllables in the *Yajurveda* and the *Sàmaveda*, taken together, again amounts to 432,000. In the words of Luis González

Reimann (1988), "[s]i el 432,000 es un número babilónico, es también un número védico" (103). Besides, when anyone anywhere operates simultaneously with the numbers 12 and 36, be it 12,000 verses of 36 syllables, or years of 12 months and 360 days, one is bound to encounter the number 432 followed by a number of zeros.

At this point we must raise the question: if the concept of cyclical time and world ages was indigenous to India, prior to the works of the philosophers and the astronomers, when and where did it originate?

As mentioned earlier, the *yuga/kalpa* system, as described here, is absent in the Vedic texts. Yet, being absent from the Vedic *texts* is not necessarily equivalent with being absent in Vedic *times*. In other words, although the *yuga/kalpa* system is not described in the Vedic texts we should not therefore conclude that the system is post-Vedic. Vedic scholars often overlook the fact that they are dealing with a period in Indian history for which the written records are limited, to one single text for the earliest stage (the *Rigveda*), and gradually more texts, yet all issued from the same restricted socio-religious milieus. Considering these texts as representative of life in Vedic times (Bhargava 1971; Zimmer 1879) is fallacious. The Vedas never were texts of the Indian masses. The texts themselves insist that they should not even be listened to by women and *shûdras*, and many others, including brahmans, remained totally ignorant of them. It is in that large extra-Vedic space, whose beliefs were not recorded, that we are looking for the origin of cyclical time in ancient India.

First, the reason why the concept of eternal return is absent from the Vedic texts is obvious: it was opposed to some of the basic principles of Vedic Hinduism. I already referred to the term *agre* ("in the beginning"), which appears with some frequency in the Upanishads. Time does have a beginning in Vedic texts. Deussen (1920) demonstrated how Shankara needed to interpret a verse from the *Rigveda* (10.190.3): "the creator fashioned the sun and the moon *yathàpurvam*," not with its obvious meaning "one after the other," but with the meaning "as before" (199).

Conversely, as far as "the end" is concerned, Vedic Hinduism is a system of escape, of liberation (*mukti* or *moksha*) from the physical world (cf. Gonda 1948; Trautmann 1995). The doctrine of *karma*, in which one's status in future lives is determined by the actions performed in prior existences, may lead to temporary lapses, but its ultimate goal is to set every *àtman* free, to have it absorbed into *brahma*, liberate it from the cycle of death and rebirth (*sansàra*), and bring its earthly existence to an end. Time is not endless in the Vedas.

Second, even though the Vedic texts do not describe any system of cyclical time, they exhibit a large number of passages which clearly allude to it (Muir 1967:43-49). For each of these passages scholars have engaged in endless controversies on whether the Vedic composers knew cyclical time or not. Their conclusions range from total acceptance to total denial. This chapter can only present a couple of examples, in chronological order (as far as this is possible with Indian texts). Even in the *Rigveda* the term *yuga* (*yugám*) indicates not only a yoke (Latin *iugum*, Greek *zugón*), but also periods of time, three years, five years, etc., including four instances where *yuga* is qualified by the adjective *mânusha* ("human"). The terms *krita*, *tretà*, *dvàpara*, and *àskanda* (not *kali*) appear in the *Yajurveda* but seem to refer to the game of dice. From the *Atharvaveda* onward the picture becomes more confused. A sequence "one hundred years, an *ayuta*,* two *yugas*, three, four" (8.2.21) has led to endless and inconclusive disputations, and even more so a passage from the *Aitareyabràhmana*: "Kali he becometh who lieth, Dvàpara when he riseth, Tretà when he standeth erect, And Krta when he moveth" (7.15) (Keith 1920:302). Passages in the Upanishads do contain the terms *krita* (*Chàndogya Upanishad* 4.1.4, 4.1.6, and 4.3.8) and *tretà* (*Mândûkya Upanishad* 1.2.1) but are too obscure to decide in either direction. Only in the late *Shvetâshvatara Upanishad* is there a reference to world creation and world destruction (3.2 and 4.1), perhaps

---

* Ayuta is a word-number for 10,000, i.e., 100 · 100; consequently *yuga* might then amount to 10,000 · 100, or even 10,000 · 10,000 years.

to repeated creation and destruction (5.3), but even here interpretations vary.

The logical approach to these Vedic texts is not to attempt to determine whether or not their composers knew or accepted the system of world periods and eternal return, rather to conclude that they alluded to them, but did not accept them because they were ireconcilable with more basic Vedic concepts. Note that the school of Indian philosophy most concerned with a correct interpretation of the Veda, Mîmânsâ, is the only one that explicitly rejects the concept of cyclical time: the Mîmânsâ concept of an eternally existing Veda is incompatible with periodic world destruction.

On the other hand, the most numerous and most detailed descriptions of cyclical time appear in the *Puràṇas*. According to Willibald Kirfel (1927), the very structure of the *Puràṇas* cannot be properly understood unless it is seen against the background of world creations and world destructions (xvii). In his commentary on the *Rigveda*, Sàyana clearly states that, women and *shûdras* being barred from access to the true Veda, "the *puràṇas* are the Vedas for women and *shûdras* " (L. Rocher 1986:16). The *puràṇas* are "the scriptures of popular Hinduism" (Raghavan 1953; Rocher 1986:16). Understandably, this popular literature, originating outside the limited circle of the Vedic practitioners, as we have it on our book shelves, is far more recent than the Vedas. The idea that the materials contained in the *puràṇas* are not merely recent, and representative of later sectarian Hinduism only was first put forth by Vans Kennedy (1831) (against Wilson 1972:iii–iv; see also Burnouf 1840:viii-ix; Chaudhuri 1929). By now, there is general agreement that many materials incorporated in the relatively recent *puràṇas* are, in fact, old, even as old as the Vedas. Given the oblique references to cyclical time in the Vedas on the one hand, and the detailed descriptions in the *puràṇas* on the other, we suggest that the concept of cyclical time in India originated in extra-Vedic "popular" beliefs in early, possibly Vedic, times. Similarly, Oskar von Hinüber (1994) convincingly argued in favor of an oral formula tradition, which appears in

Buddhist sources, but must be much older, even though Vedic literature does not mention it (7).

The fact that world ages and cyclical time in India are old, that they did not have to wait for the writers of the philosophical schools to invent them or for the astronomers to borrow them from sources outside India, is not surprising. As Eliade states, "it would be difficult to explain why the Indo-Aryans did not also share, from the period of their common prehistory, the conception of time held by all primitives" (1949:115; also 1957:177). Given Indians' propensity to quantify, it is also not surprising that they amplified the cycles they perceived around them—day/night, seasons, years—into ever-larger cycles and that they assigned proportionately higher numbers to them. What makes Indians unique is the extent to which, at an early date, they elaborated a system of cyclical time in great detail (Eliot 1962:334; Schneider 1958:156), and the way—or ways—in which they made similar but ever larger cycles proceed from human time to divine time, and from divine time—even Brahmà's life is measured—to endless cosmic time.

References

Abegg, Emil. *Der Messiasglaube in Indien und Iran*. Berlin-Leipzig: de Gruyter, 1928.

Al-Biruni. *Alberuni's India*. Trans. Edward C. Sachau. [Orig. London 1888] Delhi: S. Chand, 1964.

Bareau, André. "The Notion of Time in Early Buddhism." *East and West* 7 (1975):353–64.

Bhargava, Purushottam L. *India in the Vedic Age* 2nd ed. Aminabad: Upper India Publishing House, 1971.

Burnouf, Eugène. *Le Bhâgavata Purâna* 1. Paris: Imprimerie Royale, 1840.

Brown, W. Norman. "Agni, Sun, Sacrifice, and Vàc." *Journal of the American Oriental Society* 88 (1968):199–218.

———. *Man in the Universe*. Berkeley, CA: University of California Press, 1966.

Bühler, Georg. *The Laws of Manu*. Oxford: Clarendon Press, 1886.

Burgess, Ebenezer, and William D. Whitney. "Translation of the Sûrya-Siddhânta." *Journal of the American Oriental Society* 6 (1860):141–498.

Carpenter, J. Estlin, ed. *Dîghanikâya* 3. Pali Text Society 67. London: Oxford University Press, 1911.

Chaudhuri, Sashi B. "Antiquity of the Puràníc Story Traditions." *Journal of Indian History* 8 (1929):1–17.

Clark, Walter E. "Science." In G. T. Garratt, *The Legacy of India*. Oxford: Clarendon Press, 1937: 335–68.

Datta, Bibhutibhushan and Avadhesh N. Singh. *History of Hindu Mathematics*. Bombay: Asia Publishing House, 1962, 1.

Deussen, Paul. *Allgemeine Geschichte der Philosophie* 1, 4th part 2. Leipzig: Brockhaus, 1920.

Dundas, Paul. *The Jains*. London: Routledge, 1991.

Eliade, Mircea. *Cosmos and History. The Myth of the Eternal Return* trans. Willard R. Trask.[Orig. *Le Mythe de l'Eternel Retour: Archétypes et Répétition*. Paris: Gallimard, 1949]. New York: Harper and Row, 1959.

———. "Time and Eternity in Indian Thought." In Joseph Campbell, ed., *Man and Time*. New York: Bollingen Foundation, 1957, 173–200.

Eliot, Charles. *Hinduism and Buddhism. An Historical Sketch*. London: Routledge & Kegan Paul [Orig. 1921] 1962, 1.

Fleet, John F. "The Kali Era of B.C. 3102." *Journal of the Royal Asiatic Society* (1911):481–96, 675–98.

Garbe, Richard. *Die Sànkhya Philosophie: Eine Darstellung des indischen Rationalismus.* Leipzig: Hassel, 1895.

Glasenapp, Helmuth von. *Der Jainismus. Eine indische Erlösungsreligion.* [Orig. Berlin 1925] Hildesheim: Georg Olm, 1964.

Gonda, Jan. "A Note on Indian Pessimism." In *Studia varia Carolo Guilielmo Volgraff a discipulis oblata (Studia Volgraff).* Amsterdam: North-Holland, 1948, 34–48.

Hinüber, Oskar von. *Untersuchungen zur Mündlichkeit früher mittelindischer Texte der Buddhisten.* Stuttgart: Steiner, 1994.

Jacobi, Hermann. "Ages of the World (Indian)." In James Hastings, ed., *Encyclopedia of Religion and Ethics* 1. Edinburgh: T. & T. Clark, 1908, 200–202.

———. *Göttingische Gelehrte Anzeigen.* 1895, 201–11.

Jahn, Karl. "The Yugas of the Indians in Islamic Historiography." *Der Islam* 33 (1957):127–34.

Jaini, Padmanabh S. *The Jaina Path of Purification.* Berkeley, CA: University of California Press, 1979.

Kane, Pandurang V. *History of Dharmasàstra* 3. Poona: Bhandarkar Oriental Research Institute, 1846.

———. *History of Dharmasàstra* 5. Poona: Bhandarkar Oriental Research Institute, 1958.

Keith, A. Berriedale. *Rigveda Brahmanas.* Harvard Oriental Series 25. Cambridge, MA: Harvard University Press, 1920.

Kennedy, Vans. *Researches into the Nature and Affinity of Ancient and Hindu Mythology.* London: Longman, 1831.

Kirfel, Willibald. *Das Purànapancalaksana. Versuch einer Textgeschichte.* Bonn: Schroeder, 1927.

———. *Die Kosmographie der Inder.* [Orig. Bonn-Leipzig 1920] Hildesheim: Georg Olm, 1967.

Kloetzli, Randy. *Buddhist Cosmology*. Delhi: Motilal Banarsidass, 1983.

La Vallée-Poussin, Louis de. "Ages of the World (Buddhism)." In James Hastings, ed., *Encyclopedia of Religion and Ethics* 1. Edinburgh: T. & T. Clark, 1908, 187–90.

Lüders, Heinrich. "Das Würfelspiel im alten Indien." *Abh. d. kgl. Ges. d.Wiss. zu Göttingen*, Phil.-Hist. Kl., N. F. 9.2, 1907.

Macdonell, Anthony A., and A. Berriedale Keith. *Vedic Index of Names and Subjects*. [Orig. London 1912] Delhi: Motilal Banarsidass, 1958, 1.

Mandal, Kumar K. *A Comparative Study of the Concepts of Space and Time in Indian Thought*. Varanasi: Chowkhamba Sanskrit Series Office, 1968.

Marshall, Peter J., ed. *The British Discovery of Hinduism in the Eighteenth Century*. Cambridge: Cambridge University Press, 1970.

Menninger, Karl. *Zahl und Ziffer. Eine Kulturgeschichte der Zahl* 2nd ed. Göttingen: Vandenhoeck & Ruprecht, 1957.

Meyer, Hans. "Die Lehre von der ewigen Wiederkehr aller Dinge." In Albert M Königer, ed., *Beiträge zur Geschichte des christlichen Altertums und der Byzantinischen Literatur. Festgabe Albert Ehrhard*. [Orig. Bonn-Leipzig: Schroeder, 1922] Amsterdam: Rodopi, 1969, 359–80.

Mill, James. *The History of British India* 4th ed. Notes and Annotations by Horace H. Wilson. London: James Madden, 1840, 1.

Muir, John. "Account of the System of Yugas, Manvantaras amd Kalpas." In *Original Sanskrit Texts* 2nd ed. [Orig. London: 1891] Amsterdam: Oriental Press, 1967.

Neugebauer, Otto. *The Exact Sciences of Antiquity* 2nd ed. Providence, RI: Brown University Press, 1957.

Pingree, David. "Astronomy and Astrology in India and Iran." *Isis* 54 (1963):229–46.

———. "History of Mathematical Astronomy in India." In Charles C. Gillespie, ed., *Dictionary of Scientific Biography* 1. New York: Scribner, 1978b, 533–633.

———, ed., *TheYavanajàtaka of Sphujidhvaja*. Cambridge, MA: Harvard University Press, 1978a, 1.

Pisani, Vittore. "Wortgeschichliche Späne, II." *Zeitschrift der deutschen morgenländischen Gesellschaft* 97 (1943):325–26.

Pusalker, Achut D. *Studies in the Epics and Puràṇas*. Bombay: Bharatiya Vidya Bhavan, 1955.

Raghavan, Venkataram. "Introduction to the Hindu Scriptures." In Kenneth W. Morgan, ed., *The Religion of the Hindus*. New York: Ronald Press, 1953, 265–76.

Reimann, Luis González. *Tiempo cíclico y eras del mundo en la India*. Mexico City: El Collegio de México, 1988.

Rocher, Ludo. *The Puràṇas*. Wiesbaden: Harrassowitz, 1986.

Rocher, Rosane. *Orientalism, Poetry, and the Millennium:The Checkered Life of Nathaniel Brassey Halhed 1751–1830*. Delhi: Motilal Banarsidass, 1983.

Röck, F. "Die platonische Zahl und der babylonische Ursprung des indischen Yuga-Systems." *Zeitschrift für Assyriologie* 24 (1910):318–30.

Schayer, Stanislaw. *Contributions to the Study of Time in Indian Philosophy*. Krakow: Polish Academy, 1938.

Schneider, Ulrich. "Indisches Denken und sein Verhältnis zur Geschichte." *Saeculum* 9 (1958):156–62.

Sewell, Robert, and S. B. Dikshit. *The Indian Calendar*. London: Allen & Unwin, 1896.

Sharma, R. S. "The Kali Age: A Period of Social Crisis." In S. N. Mukherjee, ed., *India: History and Thought. Essays in Honour of A. L. Basham*. Calcutta: Subarnarekha, 1982, 186–203.

Shukla, Kripa S., ed., *Aryabhatiya of Aryabhata*. New Delhi: Indian National Science Academy, 1976, 2.

Stevenson, Margaret. *The Heart of Jainism*. London: Oxford University Press, 1915.

Thibaut, Georg. *Astronomie, Astrologie und Mathematik*. Strassburg: Trübner, 1899.

Trautmann, Thomas R. "Indian Time, European Time." In Diane O. Hughes and Thomas R. Trautmann, eds., *Time: Histories and Ethnologies*. Ann Arbor, MI: University of Michigan Press, 1995, 167–97.

van der Waerden, Bartel L. "The Great Year in Greek, Persian and Hindu Astronomy." *Archive for History of Exact Sciences* 18 (1977/78):359–83.

———. "Das grosse Jahr und die ewige Wiederkehr." *Hermes* 80 (1952):129–55.

Wackernagel, Jacob. *Altindische Grammatik* 3. Göttingen: Vandenhoeck & Ruprecht, 1930.

Warren, Henry C. *Buddhism in Translations*. Cambridge, MA: Harvard University Press, 1896.

Weber, Albrecht. "Vedische Angaben über Zeittheilung und hohe Zahlen." *Zeitschrift der deutschen morgenländischen Gesellschaft* 15 (1861):132–40.

Wilson, Horace H. *Visnu Puràna*. [Orig. London 1840] Calcutta: Punthi Pustak, 1972.

Yadava, B. N. S. "The Accounts of the Kali Age and the Social Transition from Antiquity to the Middle Ages." *The Indian Historical Review* 5 (1979):31–63.

Zimmer, Heinrich. *Altindisches Leben*. Berlin: Weidmann, 1879.

• • 5 • •

CYCLICAL AND TELEOLOGICAL
TIME IN THE HEBREW BIBLE

Marc Brettler

In the middle of the 20th century there was a common perception that biblical time is fundamentally different in nature from time as it was understood in classical antiquity. The contrast was often drawn between biblical teleological time—time that is oriented toward the end or completion, and Greek cyclical time (Curtis 1963; Brettler 1995). Most scholars have moved away from this simple typology to appreciate that in both civilizations there were a variety of conceptions of time. We shall attempt to outline ancient Israelite notions of time as reflected in the Hebrew Bible. One of the major changes of biblical scholarship since the 1980s, partially under the influence of feminism, is an appreciation of the difference between biblical Israel (Israel as it is reflected in the Bible) and ancient Israel. The latter reflects a much broader group of people than what is reflected in the Bible (Zevit 2001). Most significantly, there is a recognition that the Bible by and large reflects elite rather than popular perspectives and that it is thus not prudent to generalize from the Bible to ancient Israel as a whole. We shall also suggest, somewhat paradoxically, that the notions of cyclical and teleological time are not as contradictory as they might seem.

It is not easy to summarize the biblical notion(s) of time. The Hebrew Bible is a complex anthology produced over a millennium, with the earliest part usually considered to be the Song of Deborah, from the 12th pre-Christian century while parts of the book of Daniel reflect the 2nd pre-Christian century. It is unlikely that all biblical authors during this long time period had the same notions of time. Furthermore, given that most biblical literature predates the Greek introduction of second-order thinking, which may only be found in Ecclesiastes (Machinist 1995), there are few theoretical comments about time in the Bible (Barr 1961). We shall begin with the most explicit discussion of time, from the book of Ecclesiastes, most probably a late 3rd century biblical book (Crenshaw 1992; Machinist 1995; Seow 1997), which does contain explicit reflections about cyclical time. These reflections will frame an exposition of other biblical texts.

Ecclesiastes is one of the few biblical books to contain the word זְמָן ("time" in modern Hebrew), a word borrowed from the Aramaic זִמְנָא (Koehler and Baumgartner 1994). The more common biblical word for "time," typically used for a specific time, is עֵת. An analysis of the distribution of this word in Ecclesiastes relative to the rest of the Bible shows that it is literally off the charts—עֵת, cited 40 times, comprises nearly .9% of the words in that book. Of course many of these occurrences are in the famous chapter 3:

> (1) A time (זְמָן) is set for everything, a time (עֵת) for every experience under heaven: (2) A time (עֵת) for being born and a time (עֵת) for dying, a time (עֵת) for planting and a time (עֵת) for uprooting the planted; (3) a time for slaying and a time for healing, a time for tearing down and a time for building up; (4) a time for weeping and a time for laughing, a time for wailing and a time for dancing; (5) a time for throwing stones and a time for gathering stones, a time for embracing and a time for shunning embraces; (6) a time for seeking and a time for losing, a time for keeping and a time

for discarding; (7) a time for ripping and a time for sewing, a time for silence and a time for speaking; (8) a time for loving and a time for hating; a time for war and a time for peace. (*Tanakh* 1985, slightly modified)

The word עת appears throughout the book as well (see 3:11, 17; 7:17; 8:5, 6, 9; 9:8, 11, 12 (2x); 10:17). Its use in chapter 3 is exactly the opposite of that seized upon by the anti-war movement. It does not mean that through human effort we can determine that it is a time for peace rather than a time for war; instead, it suggests that God determines these times. In the words of Ecclesiastes 3:9–11, words that never made it into Pete Seeger's famous song, "(9) What value, then, can the man of affairs get from what he earns? (10) I have observed the business that God gave man to be concerned with: (11) He brings everything to pass precisely at its time; He also puts eternity in their mind, but without man ever guessing, from first to last, all the things that God brings to pass."

In other words, God controls the cycles of events, comprised of each event and its opposite. People are created with a desire to understand these cycles, but as the previous verses emphasize, that desire is futile.

With the exception of some of its final verses, which likely reflect a pious reworking of the main ideas of Ecclesiastes, the book is typically considered to be an editorial unity though, since it incorporates earlier material, it should not be considered the composition of a single individual (Crenshaw 1992:272–73). The opening of the book, which should be connected to chapter 3, is one of the strongest statements of periodicity (1:4–9):

(4) One generation goes, another comes, but the earth remains the same forever. (5) The sun rises, and the sun sets—and glides back to where it rises. (6) Southward blowing, turning northward, ever turning blows the wind; on its rounds the wind returns. (7) All streams flow into the

sea, yet the sea is never full; to the place from which they flow the streams flow back again. (8) All such things are wearisome: No man can ever state them; the eye never has enough of seeing, nor the ear enough of hearing. (9) Only that shall happen which has happened, only that occur which has occurred; there is nothing new beneath the sun!

Humanity is powerless before this divinely controlled periodicity; this explains why the philosopher believes (1:2–3): "(2) Utter futility!—said Koheleth—Utter futility! All is futile! (3) What real value is there for a man in all the gains he makes beneath the sun?" Chapter 3:10–11, which states that God gave people the desire to figure out the future, with no success, adds to this feeling of futility: events repeat, and the general principles of these repetitions are noted by people, but they are incompletely understood, and humans cannot determine their specifics.

The idea of periodicity of events is reflected in a variety of other, earlier texts as well. For example, Jeremiah 5:24 notes that God could be understood as the One "who gives the rain, the early and late rain in season" (Fox 1999:199). This notion is based on the climate of Israel, which is extremely predictable, with a rainy season stretching from October through March (Frick 1992:122–25). It is extremely rare for it to rain from May to September. Such cycles, which determined all agricultural activities, were quite obvious to the ancient Israelite. In fact, the earliest extra-biblical Hebrew document, the Gezer calendar, a pottery shard most likely from the 10th century, lists 8 periods of one or two months each and characterizes each through an agricultural activity: "months of vintage and olive harvest; months of sowing; months of spring pasture; month of flax pulling; month of barley harvest; month of wheat harvest and measuring; months of pruning; month of summer fruit" (Gibson 1973:2; see also McCarter 2000:222). Though not all phenomena should be reduced to environmental issues (Thompson 1999:155–58), it seems obvious that a civilization that develops in an area with stark, clearly observable weather patterns that determine sustenance might view the world more generally through cycles.

This understanding may have influenced the authors of some biblical texts, who depicted specific events in a cyclical or periodic fashion, as they gave a narrative shape to the (perceived) past (Brettler 1995). These historians, who lived in the 6th century before the time of Ecclesiastes, were not thinking in abstract terms of time as cyclical as they composed the Deuteronomistic History—Deuteronomy, Joshua, Judges, Samuel, and Kings. Nevertheless, the manner in which historical events are depicted in this large work is important and *may* have a bearing on a society's understanding of time (see Muntz 1977:223 cautioning about a society's ideas about determining the past from their historical narratives).

These cycles are most explicit in the biblical book of Judges, which depicts the history after the "conquest" of Canaan, described in the book of Joshua (Dever 1990:37–84), and before the rise of the monarchy, described in Samuel. The history of the composition of Judges is quite complex and is made even more complicated by the fact that it is both a self-standing book and, according to scholarly theories, is part of Deuteronomistic History (McKenzie 1992:160–168; Campbell and O'Brien 2000). These five books—Samuel and Kings are a single book in the Hebrew tradition but are split into two in the Septuagint tradition, which is followed by the Vulgate and the English tradition—were brought together by an ancient editor who was part of the Deuteronomistic school. In other words, these books share the ideology, theology, and vocabulary of the book of Deuteronomy, which ultimately formed the introduction to the Deuteronomistic history. This is not a technical, trivial hypothesis, but a strong theory which suggests that a discussion of periodicity in Judges should also look at the place of this phenomenon in the larger work.

The major section of Judges (Brettler 2002), comprised of the middle of chapter two through the end of chapter 16, is characterized by cycles. What is so very unusual about this is that these cycles are (1) extensive; (2) mentioned explicitly throughout the book; and (3) introduced through the verb ויוסיפו "they again" (see 3:12; 4:1; 10:6; 13:1). They are first presented in a paradigm in 2:11–19 (see Becker 1990:83, Lindars 1995:100, and Greenspahn 1986 for slightly differing outlines of the paradigm):

> (11) And the Israelites did what was offensive to the Lord. They worshiped the Baalim (12) and forsook the Lord, the God of their fathers, who had brought them out of the land of Egypt. They followed other gods, from among the gods of the peoples around them, and bowed down to them; they provoked the Lord. (13) They forsook the Lord and worshiped Baal and the Ashtaroth. (14) Then the Lord was incensed at Israel, and He handed them over to foes who plundered them. He surrendered them to their enemies on all sides, and they could no longer hold their own against their enemies. (15) In all their campaigns, the hand of the Lord was against them to their undoing, as the Lord had declared and as the Lord had sworn to them; and they were in great distress. (16) Then the Lord raised up chieftains [others "judges"] who delivered them from those who plundered them. (17) But they did not heed their chieftains either; they went astray after other gods and bowed down to them. They were quick to turn aside from the way their fathers had followed in obedience to the commandments of the Lord; they did not do right. (18) When the Lord raised up chieftains for them, the Lord would be with the chieftain and would save them from their enemies during the chieftain's lifetime; for the Lord would be moved to pity by their moanings because of those who oppressed and crushed them. (19) But when the chieftain died, they would again act basely, even more than the preceding generation—following other gods, worshiping them, and bowing down to them; they omitted none of their practices and stubborn ways.

This cycle ends where it begins. Chapters 3–16 then illustrate it with a depiction of six judges—called major judges (Brettler 2002:22–23)—or chieftains: Othniel, Ehud, Deborah-Barak, Gideon, Jephtah, and Samson. These are called major judges by scholars. Though each major judge narrative is very different in size and style, each contains some of the language also found in the paradigm in chapter 2, and each illustrates the pattern of that paradigm. For example, the story of Gideon begins: "Then the Israelites did what was offensive to the LORD, and the LORD delivered them into the hands of the Midianites for seven years" (6:1). It then describes this subjugation in some detail, noting: "Israel was reduced to utter misery by the Midianites, and the Israelites cried out to the LORD" (v. 6). Gideon is then commissioned as a judge, and he defeats the enemy. The story concludes: "Thus Midian submitted to the Israelites and did not raise its head again; and the land was tranquil for forty years in Gideon's time" (8:28). The other five stories about the major judges have the same structure and use much of the same vocabulary.

Periodicity is evident elsewhere in the book as well. In addition to the judges mentioned above, about whom we have detailed narratives, chapters 10 and 12 list leaders—called minor judges (Brettler 2002:22–23)—with little information. It is uncertain whether these judges had a different function than the major judges or if they had a similar function and may have been known to the editor through a different source (see the studies of Mullen and Lemche at Brettler 2002:22). What is significant is how highly structured this list is: many of these entries share the structure "After X son of Y son of Z/him, a man A, arose to deliver/judge Israel. He lived at B in C. He judged Israel for D years; then he died and was buried at E." The variables, X, Y, Z, A–E are often different, but the structure of the list, especially within the structure of Judges, suggests strong periodicity.

The last five chapters of Judges, 17–21, do not depict judges of either the major or minor type; instead, they are often seen (perhaps incorrectly) as an appendix (Brettler 2002: 80). They too exhibit periodicity, especially through the refrain which appears in each of the two horrific stories narrated. This refrain appears once in each in the short form "In those days there was no king in Israel" (Judges 18:1; 19:1) and once each in the long form which supplements the earlier statement with "each man did as he pleased" (Judges 17:6; 21:25). Finally, given all of these repetitions and cycles, it is tempting to read the introduction to the book, especially the successive notes in chapter one that tribe after tribe did not succeed in dispossessing the natives of the land (Judges 1:19, 21, 27, 28, 29, 30, 31, 32, 33) as cyclical as well (Brettler 2002:92–102).

Cycles predominate in the book of Judges, appearing in all sections of the book. The book's author clearly believed that history repeats itself and in that sense believed in cyclical time. Events are like the seasons and times of Ecclesiastes, like the weather of ancient Israel noted in Jeremiah, which has a clear structure, though it is open to some internal variation. Similarly, the judges are all depicted in a similar fashion, though they do not all behave in exactly the same manner or defeat the same enemy.

The structure of Judges as a set of cycles is unique and is not repeated elsewhere in the Deuteronomistic history. This is especially striking in Joshua, where it would have been easy to depict the conquest of Canaan as a set of recurring, similar conquests of smaller parts of the land, but this is not done. Some obvious patterns appear in Samuel and Kings—for example, a cycle of David fleeing from Saul at the end of Second Samuel (Brettler 2002:13–15), or a very vague pattern of good and bad kings in Kings (Trompf 1979:227), but there is no pattern as tight as the one found *explicitly* in Judges. There are several cases of what Trompf (1979) calls recurrence, what others might call typology (Brettler 1995), but there are no cycles comparable to those found in Judges. Certain patterns which scholars find, for example, "the recurrent pattern of failure and grace" (Trompf 1979a:222) are either overly schematic or Christian, or both.

It is possible that Deuteronomy is attempting to suggest that there would be a pattern of Moses-like prophets succeeding one another: "I will raise up a prophet for them from among their own people, like yourself: I will put My words in his mouth and he will speak to them all that I command him" (18:18). Wilson (1980:155–156) speaks of a succession of prophets holding the office of a Mosaic prophet. Thus, within the Deuteronomistic history, Joshua succeeds Moses (Deuteronomy 34:9) (Römer and Brettler 2000), and Elisha succeeds Elijah (1 Kings 19:19; 2 Kings 2:13–15) (McKenzie 1991), but this is hardly worked out in the detail of the cyclical pattern like the one found in Judges. Incidentally, it should not be surprising that this idea of cycles is unique to Judges, since that book is unique in other ways as well, including its focus on women (Bellis 1994:112–139; Ackerman 1998), and its depiction of that period as a unique period of divine grace in which God forgives Israel time and time again even though his people do not repent (Greenspahn 1986).

Cases of recurrence may be found outside the Deuteronomistic history (Knopper 2001), but here too none of these is as structured as Judges. For example, the book of Genesis is often read as a succession of experiments: first Adam and his descendents are chosen, but this fails, so Noah and his descendents are chosen, but this fails, and then Abram is chosen (Westerman 1984:66–67). This structure, however, is not clearly marked in the text. Certain events repeat themselves in Genesis three times. For example, in chapters 12, 20, and 26, a patriarch attempts to pass his wife off as his sister (Brettler 1995:51–52). Such repetitions appear in other books as well. As we have seen, 2 Samuel 24 and 26 both tell stories of David fleeing from Saul, having the ability to kill him, but not killing "the Lord's anointed." In both stories Saul calls David "my father." Essentially, the same event happens twice, in different places, with slightly different narrative details. It is likely that the existence of the idea of historical recurrence allowed, perhaps even encouraged, the redactors of these texts to incorporate variant traditions so it would seem that events were recurring.

The same is true of typologies found throughout the Bible, but especially in books like Chronicles (Brettler 1995:27). However, none of these recurrences is marked by a paradigm in the same way that Judges is, nor do any have several cases of recurrence beginning with the word ויסיפו, "they again" as in Judges. A more complete study would uncover different notions of recurrence, from simple typologies (Trompf 1979a:213), where an event is repeated once, through the full-blown, six-fold cycle with an introductory paradigm found in Judges. In any case, it is clear that recurrence does exist in a range of biblical texts.

As noted earlier, cyclical time is typically contrasted with linear, teleological time. Since the 19th century, this period has been called the *eschaton*, derived from the Greek *eschatos*, a word that may mean the "farthest extent in space, final element of time, and last piece of money" (Petersen 1992:576). This modern convention is based on early Greek translations in the Septuagint (Marcos 2000), for the Hebrew אחרית הימים, often translated as the "end of days" but under Septuagint influence translated in the King James version as "last days." The use of the term *eschaton* and related terms such as "eschatology" prejudges the situation, suggesting that there is an end of time. Thus native terms for what may be more neutrally called the ideal future must be studied to see the extent to which this period is conceived of as an end and the extent to which earlier time periods are viewed as inextricably leading up to it.

The terminology used for describing this ideal future *never* refers to the end of time. This is even the case for time as it is depicted in the Dead Sea Scrolls (Brin 2001:219–367; Collins 1997:52–72; Collins 2000). The scrolls are much more concerned with eschatology and have a much more developed sense of eschatology than all texts from the Hebrew Bible except for Daniel which shows greater affinity to the Dead Sea Scrolls than to much of the rest of the Hebrew Bible (Collins 1997:12–18).

A common term found in prophetic literature is the Day of the Lord (Hebrew יום יהוה). Given the wide distribution of this term over a long time period, the understanding of this Day is not stable, but in general it describes a day in which YHWH, the Israelite God, is manifest in the world as warrior, sometimes fighting against Israel, sometimes against Israel's and His enemies (Paul 1991:182–184). The term appears 16 times (Saebø 1990:29). Much more frequent is the term יום ההוא "that day." It, too, appears in a variety of contexts, though it is favored in certain prophetic books, especially Isaiah (Saebø 1990:16). The phrase is often used, especially in non-prophetic literature, in its plain sense, referring to a day mentioned earlier in the narrative (but see Saebø 1990:30), but it also has a technical, prophetic usage referring to a particular time period. It often seems to refer to the Day of the LORD (Saebø 1990:30).

It is unlikely that these terms refer to the eschatological period since Hebrew יום in the singular means "a day," and is not generally delexicalized in the sense of a broader period of time. The expected plural of יום ההוא ("that day") is ימים ההם/ההמה ("those days"). This expression is attested in the Hebrew Bible in both a plain (Judges 21–25) and a technical sense, but the technical sense of an ideal future *period* is rare and is largely confined to Jeremiah (3:16, 18; 5:18; 31:29, 33; 33:15; 50:4, 20; Joel 3:2; 4:1; Zechariah 8:6, 10, 23). Here too, none of these contexts suggests that this time is an end, since "those days" initiate a long time-period. In other contexts ימים, "days," without any pronoun, may also refer to the ideal future. For example, a secondary addition (Wolff 1977:352–354; Jeremias 1998:162) concluding the book of Amos describing restored Israel and idealized agricultural productivity is introduced הנה ימים באים, "Look—days are coming." The conclusion of Amos, for example, suggests a long continuing period. However, there is nothing in any of these contexts to suggest that these days were viewed as an end.

The most familiar term that in the popular perception is related to eschatology is the English "end of days." This English term, however, is an incorrect translation from the Hebrew אחרית הימים,

a mistranslation dating from the time of the Septuagint. It is better translated "in the days to come" (Collins 2000:370–72). This may be seen most clearly from Genesis 49:1, which introduces the blessings of the patriarch Jacob, in which he tells his children the fate of their tribes באחרית הימים. The information conveyed is about the monarchical period (Speiser 1964), and certainly not about a final period. Its use in prophetic contexts bears this out.

The most famous "eschatological" prophecy using the term אחרית הימים is from Isaiah 2. It states that in אחרית הימים the Jerusalem Temple will be central, all nations will go there to get divine instruction, and, most famously, "and they shall beat their swords into plowshares and their spears into pruning hooks: nation shall not take up sword against nation; they shall never again know war" (2:4; see also Micah 5.3; Blenkinsopp 2000:190). This is a prophecy that is meant to transpire in the future, באחרית הימים, but there is nothing to suggest that this is the "end of time" (Steudel 1993; Martinez and Tigchalaar 1997:100).

In fact, even more revolutionary notions of what scholars call the eschatological period do not imply an end of time. One such radical notion is found at the end of Isaiah 65:17, describing a creation of a new heaven and earth (Childs 2001:439–49). The anonymous prophet clearly views this as a crucial event, but it is very much in time—according to the following chapter, after this new creation, "and new moon after new moon, And Sabbath after Sabbath, all flesh shall come to worship Me—said the LORD" (66:22). These events that follow this new creation are very much in, and not at the end of, time.

In sum, those who depict biblical time as linear, with the "end of time" as a goal or *telos*, are misreading the text. Prophetic literature presents a set of traditions that describe an ideal future that in some distinctive ways—agriculturally, or in terms of world peace, or in terms of animal behavior—will be fundamentally different. But this is depicted as a long period, in which life is otherwise normal. Furthermore, it is typically unclear if this period is to last forever.

Finally, it is noteworthy that even this type of eschatology is not predominant in the Bible. It is certainly strong in most prophetic traditions, but it is absent from Torah, historical books, Psalms, and the wisdom strands, which make up the majority of biblical texts (Petersen 1992:579). Stated differently, eschatological views do not predominate in the Hebrew Bible, and even when they appear, they are not eschatological in the etymological sense, suggesting an end.

Even when this period is depicted as radically different than the author's own period, it is often phrased not as a new final era, but as a return to the old. This fundamental observation was made by the great late 19th and early 20th century German Bible scholar, Hermann Gunkel (1895), who observed that the end of time is depicted as the beginning of time. Thus in Isaiah 65–66, explored above, the ideal future is portrayed as a re-creation, where Genesis is reenacted, and a new heavens and earth are fashioned (Fishbane 1985:354–356). Similarly, another well-known prophetic "eschatological" text, Jeremiah 31:31, set אחרי הימים ההם ("after those days") notes: "See, a time is coming (הנה ימים באים)—declares the LORD—when I will make a new covenant with the House of Israel and the House of Judah." This vision of the future as well is not viewed as something totally new, but as a reworking of the covenant given to the Israelites at Sinai, but in a new form where it will be so preprogrammed in every Israelite, so he or she will follow it automatically (Carasik 1996). Here too, the future—not really the end—is based on the past.

This notion, quite literally, brings us full circle, creating a certain irony. There is no end of time (Greenberg 1983:145–47; Collins 1993:337–38; Brin 2001:264–76; Talmon 1993), but the texts that describe the future often do so in terms of the past, and thus view events as cyclical, or at least as recurring. In fact, Petersen (1992) has summarized Israelite eschatological tradition by suggesting that it is based on the patriarchal promise traditions of Genesis, the David-Zion tradition concerning the centrality of the Davidic monarch and the Jerusalem Temple, and Sinai covenant traditions concerning the revelation of law on the mountain. Thus a broad range of eschatological notions is really based on a broad range of traditions about Israel's early history.

It is difficult to talk about time as an abstraction since second-order thinking was a late arrival during the biblical period. Thus, it is not surprising that there is no extended philosophical reflection on time and its nature. Ecclesiastes offers some thoughts and suggests periodicity of events, and perhaps even a notion of cyclical time. This idea is seen clearly in the book of Judges and in some other biblical passages, though it does not typify the Deuteronomistic History as a whole. Cyclical time, however, should not be contrasted with teleological eschatological time. There is no "end of time" according to the Bible. There are, however, various depictions of the idealized future, and these are typically based on depictions of the distant past. A cycle or, at the very least, a circle is created, through which the past and future meet. This suggests that at least for some biblical tradents, the notions of cyclical and teleological time are not as mutually contradictory as we might have thought (Gould 1987:16; Zerubavel 1981:112–13).

References

Ackerman, Susan. *Warrior, Dancer, Seductress, Queen:Women in Judges and Biblical Israel*. Anchor Bible Reference Library. New York: Doubleday, 1998.

Barr, James. *The Semantics of Biblical Language*. New York: Oxford University Press, 1961, 102–104.

Becker, Uwe. *Richterzeit and Königtum: Redaktionsgeschechtlich Studien zum Richterbuch*. Beihefte zur Zeitschrift für die alttestamentliche Wissenschaft 192. Berlin: de Gruyter, 1990.

Bellis, Alice Ogden. *Helpmates, Harlots, and Heroes:Women's Stories in the Hebrew Bible*. Louisville, KY: Westminster/John Knox, 1994.

Blenkinsopp, Joseph. "Isaiah 1–39." *Anchor Bible* 19. Garden City, NY: Doubleday, 2000.

Brettler, Marc Zvi. *The Book of Judges*. Old Testament Readings. London: Routledge, 2002.

———. *The Creation of History in Ancient Israel*. London: Routledge, 1995.

Brin, Gershon. *The Concept of Time in the Bible and the Dead Sea Scrolls*. Leiden: Brill, 2001.

Campbell, Antony F., and Mark A. O'Brien. *Unfolding the Deuteronomistic History: Origins, Upgrades, Present Text*. Minneapolis, MN: Fortress Press, 2000.

Carasik, Michael A. "Theologies of Mind in Biblical Israel." Ph.D. dissertation, Brandeis University, 1996.

Childs, Brevard S. *Isaiah*. Old Testament Library. Louisville, KY: Westminster/John Knox, 2001.

Collins, John J. *Apocalypticism in the Dead Sea Scrolls*. Literature of the Dead Sea Scrolls. London: Routledge, 1997.

———. *Daniel*. Hermeneia Commentary. Minneapolis, MN: Fortress Press, 1993.

———. "Eschatology." In Lawrence H. Schiffman and James C. Vanderkam, eds., *Encyclopedia of the Dead Sea Scrolls*. Oxford: Oxford University Press, 2000, 256–61.

Crenshaw, James L. "Ecclesiastes." *Anchor Bible Dictionary 2*. New York: Doubleday, 1992.

Curtis, John Briggs. "A Suggested Interpretation of Biblical Philosophy of History." *Hebrew Union College Annual* 34 (1963):115–23.

Dever, W. G. *Recent Archaeological Discoveries and Biblical Research*. Seattle, WA: University of Washington Press, 1990.

Fishbane, Michel. *Biblical Interpretation in Ancient Israel*. Oxford: Clarendon, 1985.

Fox, Michael V. *A Time to Tear Down and A Time to Build Up: A Rereading of Ecclesiastes*. Grand Rapids, MI: Eerdmans, 1999.

Frick, Frank S. "Palestine." *Anchor Bible Dictionary* 5. New York: Doubleday, 1992.

Gibson, John C. L. *Textbook of Syrian Semitic Inscriptions:Volume 1: Hebrew and Moabite Inscriptions*. Oxford: Clarendon, 1973.

Gould, Stephen Jay. *Time's Arrow, Time's Cycle: Myth and Metaphor in the Discovery of Geological Time*. Cambridge: Cambridge University Press, 1987.

Greenberg, Moshe. "Ezekiel 1–20." *Anchor Bible* 22. New York: Doubleday, 1983.

Greenspahn, Frederick E. "The Theology of the Framework of Judges." *Vetus Testamentum* 36 (1986):285–396.

Gunkel, Hermann. *Schöpfung und Chaos in Urzeit und Endzeit*. Göttingen: Vandenhoeck & Ruprecht, 1895.

Jeremias, Jörg. *Amos*. Louisville, KY: Westminster/John Knox, 1998.

Koehler, Ludwig, and Walter Baumgartner. *The Hebrew and Aramaic Lexicon of the Old Testament*. Leiden: Brill, 1994.

Knoppers, Gary N. "Rethinking the Relationship between Deuteronomy and the Deuteronomistic History: The Case of Kings." *Catholic Biblical Quarterly* 63 (2001):393–415.

Lindars, Barnabas. *Judges 1–5: A New Translation and Commentary*. Edinburgh: T & T Clark, 1995.

Machinist, Peter. "Fate, *Miqreh*, and Reason: Some Reflections on Qohelet and Biblical Thought." In Z. Zevit, Seymour Gitin, and Michael Sokoloff, eds., *Solving Riddles and Untying Knots: Biblical, Epigraphic, and Semitic Studies in Honor of Jonah C. Greenfield*. Winona Lake, IN: Eisenbrauns, 1995, 159–75.

Marcos, Fernandez. *The Septuagint in Context: Introduction to the Greek Version of the Bible*. Leiden: Brill, 2000.

Martínez, Florentino García, and Eibert J. C. Tigchalaar, eds. *The Dead Sea Scrolls Study Edition*. Leiden: Brill, 1997, 1.

McCarter, P. Kyle. In William W. Hallo, ed., *The Context of Scripture, Vol. II: Monumental Inscriptions from the Biblical World*. Leiden:Brill, 2000.

Mckenzie, Steven L. "Deuteronomistic History." *Anchor Bible Dictionary 2*. New York: Doubleday, 1992.

———. *The Trouble with Kings: The Composition of the Book of Kings in the Deuteronomistic History*. Supplements to Vetus Testamentum 42. Leiden: Brill, 1991, 81–100.

Muntz, Peter. *The Shape of Time: A New Look at the Philosophy of History*. Middletown, CT: Wesleyan University Press, 1977.

Paul, Shalom M. "Amos." *Hermeneia*. Minneapolis, MN: Fortress Press, 1991.

Petersen, David L. "Eschatology (OT)." *Anchor Bible Dictionary 2*. New York: Doubleday, 1992.

Römer, Thomas C., and Marc Z. Brettler. "Deuteronomy 34 and the Case for a Persian Hexateuch." *Journal of Biblical Literature* 119 (2000):401–19.

Saebø, M. "יום *yôm*." G. Johannes Botterweck and Helmer Ringgren, eds., *Theological Dictionary of the Old Testament 6*. Grand Rapids, MI: Eerdmans, 1990.

Seow, Choon-Leong. "Ecclesiastes." Anchor Bible 18c. New York: Doubleday, 1997, 11–21.

Speiser, E. A. "Genesis." *Anchor Bible 1*. Garden City, NY: Doubleday, 1964.

Steudel, Annette. "'End of Days' in the Texts from Qumran." *Revue de Qumrân* 16 (1993): 225–46.

Talmon, S. "קץ *qes*." G. Johannes Botterweck and Helmer Rinngre, eds., *Theologisches Wörterbuch zum Alten Testament 7*. Stuttgart: Kohlhammer, 1993, 84–92.

Tanakh: A New Translation of the Holy Scriptures According to the Traditional Hebrew Text. Philadelphia, PA: Jewish Publication Society, 1985.

Thompson, Thomas L. *The Mythic Past: Biblical Archaeology and the Myth of Israel*. New York: Basic Books, 1999.

Trompf, G. W. *The Idea of Historical Recurrence in Western Thought: From Antiquity to the Reformation*. Berkeley, CA: University of California Press, 1979.

———. "Notions of Historical Recurrence in Classical Hebrew Historiography." Supplements to Vetus Testamentum 30 (1979):213–29.

Wilson, Robert R. *Prophecy and Society in Ancient Israel*. Minneapolis, MN: Fortress Press, 1980.

Westermann, Claus. *Genesis 1–11*. Minneapolis, MN: Augsburg, 1984.

Wolff, Hans Walter. "Joel and Amos." *Hermeneia*. Minneapolis, MN: Fortress Press, 1977.

Zerubavel, Eviatar. *Hidden Rhythms: Schedules and Calendars in Social Life*. Chicago, IL: University of Chicago Press, 1981.

Zevit, Ziony. *The Religions of Ancient Israel: A Synthesis of Parallactic Approaches*. London: Continuum, 2001.

• • 6 • •

TEMPORALITY AND THE FABRIC OF SPACE-TIME IN EARLY CHINESE THOUGHT

David W. Pankenier

Nearly fifty years ago Joseph Needham published a celebrated essay, "Time and Knowledge in China and the West," in which he surveyed Chinese ideas about time and temporality. In his magisterial overview, Needham left virtually no realm untouched in discussing time in Chinese philosophy and natural philosophy; time, chronology, and historiography; time measurement; biological change in time; concepts of social evolution and devolution; recognition of technological development over time; science and knowledge as cooperative cumulative enterprises, and more.

The subject is vast, particularly in view of the historical scope of Needham's account, which carries the story from the first historical dynasty up to the modern era. Indeed, each of the topics Needham discusses merits a monograph. My objective here is briefly to draw attention to a few of the general issues raised by Needham's conclusion concerning the position of Chinese civilization in the contrast between linear irreversible time and cyclical, recurring patterns, and then to focus on a uniquely Chinese perspective on temporality and causality.

When it comes to Chinese civilization, Needham (1981) wrote,

> Broadly speaking, and in spite of anything that has been said above, linearity . . . dominated. The apocalyptic, almost the messianic, often the evolutionary and (in its own way) the progressive, certainly the temporally linear, these elements were there, spontaneously and independently developing since the time of the Shang kingdom [1554–1046 BCE], and in spite of all that the Chinese found out or imagined about cycles, celestial or terrestrial, these were the elements that dominated the thought of Confucian scholars and the Taoist peasant-farmers. Strange as it may seem to those who still think in terms of the "timeless Orient," on the whole China was a culture more of the Irano-Judaeo-Christian type than the Indo-Hellenic. (133, 135)

One of the most important indicators leading to Needham's conclusion, though only implicit in the rationale quoted here, is his conviction, echoing the early French sinologist Marcel Granet, that the Chinese possessed a more highly developed historical sense than any other civilization (Needham and Wang 1956:289). Needham's essay generalized about the entire sweep of Chinese history. Had he restricted his discussion to the ancient period, that is, taking the Han dynasty at the beginning of the CE as his upper limit, it is unlikely he would have concluded that linearity dominated Chinese thinking about time. For example, Derk Bodde, in contrast to Needham, after exploring the same question of cyclical versus linear time in China, concludes: "Naturally, the evidence pro and con cannot be quantitatively weighed. Nonetheless, on the cyclical side, the evidence appears to me quite sufficient in quantity and clarity to justify the conclusion that, until quite recently, Chinese cyclical thinking was considerably more widespread and influential than was Chinese linear thinking" (Bodde 1991:133; see also Sivin 1966).

Of particular interest in the Chinese case, as Needham notes in discussing historical causation in the early imperial period, is "the conviction that the universe and each of the wholes composing it have a cyclical nature, undergoing alternations, so dominated [Chinese] thought that the idea of succession was always subordinated to that of interdependence. Thus retrospective explanations were not felt to involve any difficulty. 'Such and such a lord, in his lifetime, was not able to obtain the hegemony, because, after his death, human victims were sacrificed to him.' Both facts were simply part of one timeless pattern" (Needham and Wang 1956:289). Clearly, what is implicated here is hardly a conventional notion of causality, much less "historical sense" in any ordinary sense of the term, as Needham points out (Needham and Wang 1956:97).

Lawrence Fagg, like Derk Bodde, is less inclined to declare in favor of the dominance of continuous, linear time in China:

> Certainly, if only because the Chinese were such accomplished historians, they must have had a sense of linear time. This is apparent in their records of social relations and events, and is particularly evident in astronomical calculations . . . at the same time, curiously, there was a component of cyclicality in the Chinese view of political history, the successive dynasties exhibiting a periodicity in their rise and fall. There was a cyclical view also that arose from the Chinese perception of nature and the functions of the human body . . . strongly supported by Taoist concepts. It is almost as if this mixture of linear and cyclical concepts of time is another expression of the primal *yin-yang* principle, with *yang* representing linear time and *yin* cyclical time. (Fagg 1985:97)

It is no doubt a truism that no civilization has proceeded from dominantly linear to dominantly cyclical conceptions of time, rather than the other way round. Still, as Bodde's and Needham's opposing conclusions illustrate, it is no easy matter to pin down how and why a transition from the one to the other may have occurred or, more precisely, how and when the situation of relative dominance might have shifted from the one to the other of these complementary modes of experiencing time. In China, a significant factor may have been the consolidation of the imperial institution during the two centuries before the Common Era, and especially its union of convenience with Confucianism. The ascendancy of the latter, with its deep commitment to social and political history, assured that ancient and more subtle Taoist and Naturalist conceptions of pattern and phenomenological connectedness would be relegated to specialized pursuits, and with them their intense interest in timeliness, "returning" as the movement of the Tao, and especially "ideas of causality distinctly different from the Indian or Western atomistic picture in which the prior impact of one thing is the cause of the motion of another" (Needham 1981:97). In other words, the devaluation of the correlative cosmology of the Naturalists and of Taoist intuitive attunement with the timeless patterns of the cosmos meant that the synthesis of these concepts of causality and temporality, which were, strictly speaking, neither cyclical nor linear, would never be fully elaborated (see Huang and Zürcher 1995).

A famous passage from the 4th century BCE narrative history *Zuo zhuan*, now preserved as a commentary on the canonical *Spring and Autumn Annals*, offers a taste of the time-sense in the mid-1st millennium BCE.

> In the 2nd month, on day *guiwei* [20], the [dowager] marchioness Dao of Jin entertained all the men who had been engaged in the walling of Qi. A childless old man from the District of Jiang went and took his place at the feast. Some participants were dubious about his age and would have him tell it. He said, "I am a lowly person and do not know how to keep track of the years (*bu zhi ji nian*). Since the year of my birth, on day *jiazi* [1], the day of the new moon in the

first month, there have elapsed 445 *jiazi* days, and finally until today one-third of the cycle [of 60]." The officiants [of the feast] ran to the court to ask about it. Music-master Kuang said, "It was the year when Shuzhong Hui Bo of Lu had a meeting with Xi Chengzi in Chengkuang. In that year, the Di invaded Lu, and Shusun Zhuangshu defeated them at Xian, capturing their elders Qiaoru, Hui, and Pao, after all of whom he named his sons. [Hence,] it is 73 years." (Legge IX:556, modified)

Several things are noteworthy in this passage. First, more sophisticated time-keeping methods than counting the cycles of 60 are inaccessible to the free man commoner, and probably only slightly less so to other nonspecialist participants at the feast. (Note that the old man uses *ji nian*, literally "string the years," to mean "correlate the sequence of years with a record of political events/states of the world.") Second, the specialist who is in charge of record keeping at court, who is also music-master and very likely diviner as well, in the first instance places the timing of the man's birth situationally, almost as if quoting an annalistic record, and then secondarily, only after an arithmetic operation relating the continuously repeating sexagenary cycle to the civil years, is he able to fix the event chronologically.

This account is probably fairly representative and gives a good indication of the relative value attached to different kinds of temporal awareness in daily life. It also points up a central problem at the heart of temporal consciousness to which the *Book of Changes* seemed to offer a solution, as we shall see; that is, how to systematically relate subjective mental states or states of the world with an often contradictory description of the world in terms of events happening, or the "unreality of time" (Davies 2002:42).

Here is another, elite perspective on attunement as a vital concern of the ruler who aspired to achieve universal harmony and hegemony, lest his negligence or ineptitude provoke disasters. The admonition is attributed to the chief minister of the first Hegemon, Duke Huan of the state of Qi, in the 7th century BCE:

> Since mankind is one entity within nature, the one who establishes the laws must also make a study of "heavenly timeliness and earthly advantages" as a basis for devising his laws. Kuan Tzu said: "Commands have their proper times . . . . the Sage King strives to adjust to time, and to relate his governmental measures to it." Spring, summer, autumn, and winter each has its activities which should be done at those times. "When man and heaven are in accord, only then can the perfection of heaven and earth come into being." When commands and orders are not appropriate to the season, then "things undertaken will not get accomplished, and there is sure to be a great calamity." (Hsiao 1979:337)

During the last few centuries before the beginning of the present era old traditions and new speculations about the connectedness of all things were increasingly systematized and elaborated, not least by Yin-Yang correlative cosmologists, the School of Naturalists, and propounders of Taoist-inspired Lao-Huang theories of rulership. These ideas drew on ancient roots in divination methods deriving from microcosmic-macrocosmic analogies, numerology, cosmopolitical theories of cyclical dominance by the five elemental agents—wood, metal, fire, water, and earth—coupled with a highly developed sensitivity to phenomenological correspondences perceived to exist in nature. The historical sense displayed a strong bias in favor of cyclical time and historical events seen not as historical instances of human actions and motives *per se*, but in their timeless, emblematic aspect, as examples of admirable or dishonorable motives, or adherence to protocol and tradition-bound propriety. This quality of annalistic history, the beginnings of which are already discernible during Shang and Zhou a millennium earlier, is attributable to the origins of historical record keeping in the context of divination and ritualistic reporting of temporal goings-on to the ancestors.

By the early imperial period, the responsibilities of the Astrologer Royal, the official post which had evolved out of the diviners of old, encompassed everything from divination to portentology (including astrology and the interpretation of anomalous events and prodigies), to calendar making and advising on the relevance of historical precedent to current events. Rulership demanded mastery of the complex pattern of events and motives, both human and natural, in order to successfully manage their harmonization with the inchoate and constantly changing complexion of the times (Nienhauser 1994:165). Take, for example, the characterization of this enterprise by the philosopher Jia Yi, in the early 2nd century BCE:

> A popular maxim has it: "Prior events, not forgotten, teach about events to come." For this reason, in ordering the state the accomplished ruler observes the events of antiquity, tests them against the present, matches them with human affairs, examines into the principles of flourishing and decline, and looks for what is appropriate according to expediency and tendencies. In this way, discarding and adopting measures have their proper sequence, adapting and transforming their due seasons. Thus, his reign is untroubled and enduring, and his altars to the soil and grain are safeguarded. (Sima Qian 1959:6.278)

Here is the historical sense in the service of statecraft, and statecraft according to a cosmic paradigm in which the very cycles of the cosmos and the movements of Yin-Yang and the five phases are all implicated. In this world view, disturbance or disharmony at any point in the fabric of space-time or human affairs could reverberate throughout the whole, with unpredictable consequences—and not merely prospectively, but perhaps even retrospectively as we saw above. A pervasive early metaphor employed in this connection is that of a mirror, the aspiring ruler of men being enjoined to seek guidance in the image of his deeds and motives as reflected in the mirror of previous reigns as well as in the lives of his own subjects.

In attempting to grasp what this world view was like, we need to eschew conventional ideas of causality. Even words like "reverberate" or "propagate" above tend to call to mind conventional ideas of action and reaction and to invoke a presentist perspective. Rather, what is implicated here is a kind of "acausal orderedness," in which, as Needham says, the "idea of correspondence has great significance and replaces the idea of causality, for things are *connected* rather than caused." Or, in Needham's inimitable phrase, "in such a system causality is reticular and hierarchically fluctuating, not particulate and singly catenarian" (Needham and Wang 1956:289). In explaining Granet's interpretation, Needham remarks, "if two objects seemed to them to be connected, it was not by means of a cause and effect relationship, but rather 'paired' like the obverse and reverse of something, or to use a metaphor from the *Book of Changes*, like echo and sound, or shadow and light" (1956:290–91). "What Granet had in mind were *patterns simultaneously appearing in a vast field of force*, the dynamic structure of which we do not yet understand. . . . The parts, in their organizational relations, whether of a living body or of the universe, were sufficient to account, by a kind of harmony of wills, for the observed phenomena" (1956:302).

Number, too, plays a crucial role in this conception:

> In China numbers were used as qualitative instruments of order. According to Granet, the Chinese did not use numbers as quantities but as polyvalent emblems or symbols which served to express the quality of certain clusters of facts and their intrinsic hierarchical orderedness. Numbers, in their view, possess a descriptive power and thus serve as an ordering fact for "clusters of concrete objects, which they

seem to qualify merely by positioning them in space and time." In Chinese thought there is an equivalence between the essence of a thing and its position in space-time. (Needham and Wang 1956:229)

This idealized role of number achieves its highest expression in the elaborate system of the *Book of Changes* in which the 64 individual hexagrams give graphic shape to the symbolic descriptive power of numerical relations, while at the same time embodying, in their dynamic relations, the infinite changeability and creative potential of the cosmos. According to C. G. Jung:

> Number . . . is a more primitive mental element than concept. Psychologically we could define number as *an archetype of order which has become conscious*. . . . the unconscious often uses number as an ordering factor much in the same way as consciousness does. Thus numerical orders, like all other archetypal structures, can be pre-existent to consciousness and then they rather condition than are conditioned by it. Number forms an ideal *tertium comparationis* between what we usually call psyche and matter, for countable quantity is a characteristic of material phenomena *and* an irreducible *idée force* behind our mathematical reasoning. The latter consists of the "indisputability" which we experience when contemplating arrangements based on natural numbers. Thus number is a basic element in our thought processes, on the one side, and, on the other, it appears as the objective "quantity" of material objects which seem to exist independently outside our psyche." (Jung 1969:870)

Needham, the materialist, in contrast, saw the Chinese tendency to rest content with the apparent explanatory power of number as the chief impediment to further development in the philosophy of the *Book of Changes*.

As Lawrence Fagg observed: "The *I Ching (Book of Changes)* tells us that each moment can be denoted by a number indicative of the quality of that moment. Therefore, while there is in a real sense a value placed on the moments of Chinese linear time, it is not obviously goal-directed or influenced. Hence, this time also may not be easily identified with the physical world's historical arrow" (1985:155). In this regard it is also worth mentioning that some days in the cycle of 60 day-dates in continuous use since Shang times were more auspicious than others, often because of punning associations with homophones having lucky significance. Remarkably, the identity of this set of favorable and unfavorable terms persisted largely unchanged throughout the pre-imperial period from Shang through the Han. In discussing this aspect of the day-dates divined about in the late 2nd millennium BCE Shang oracle bones, David Keightley (2000) cites Clifford Geertz's observation that the Balinese "don't tell you what time it is, they tell you what kind of time it is" (33, n.55).

An illustration of the intersection of timeless pattern and dynamism in the *Book of Changes* shows how this distillation of early Chinese thinking about change and timeliness can enlighten us about views of temporality and causation as well as about certain other prefigurative metaphors in ancient Chinese thought. In the *Book of Changes*, where the tenor of the moment is a function of position, and vice versa, the concept of the right timeliness of every action is especially prominent and repeatedly stressed (Lin 1995:98). Small wonder, then, that a preoccupation with not encountering receptive times or meeting with unfavorable circumstances, seemingly preordained to frustrate one's ambitions, should have loomed large in the minds of Chinese thinkers in the late Warring States and Han periods, especially given the troubling precedent of Confucius's own failure to achieve due recognition in his day. At one point in a famous *fu* or prose poem on the theme of "Gentlemen of Integrity Unappreciated in their Time," the most influential Confucian thinker of the former Han dynasty, Dong Zhongshu (ca. 179–104 BCE), was deeply influenced by the *Book of Changes*:

> Alas, the whole world goes along with perversity! I grieve that we cannot join together in turning back.
> What else can I do but return to the constant task, and not let myself be cast about by the times.
> Though all profit be gained by violating the true self, still it is better to straighten the mind and cleave to the good.
> If only the buffeting of urgency causes me to be moved, surely I cannot be said to have an intemperate nature?
> Clearly manifesting "*Fellowship with Men*" means "*Possession in Great Measure.*"
> And to brightly show forth the "radiance of modesty," means to further the cause. (Pankenier 1990:440)

"*Tong ren*" ("Fellowship with Men") and "*Da you*" ("Possession in Great Measure") are hexagrams thirteen and fourteen in the received text of the *Book of Changes*. Their pivotal importance in the Han Confucian interpretation of the *Changes* is second only to the first two, "Qian" ("The Creative") and "Kun" ("The Receptive"), in that they symbolize, at one and the same time, the means (humanism and self-cultivation) and the end (political unity and social harmony) of the Confucian social and political agenda. In terms of their structure, there was thought to obtain an intrinsically dynamic relationship among the central ideas and images embodied in these two hexagrams, a relationship that is represented graphically in their configuration. These are two of the very few hexagrams that have a complementary pair of *Yin* and *Yang* lines occupying the two central, mutually interacting and supremely important positions in the hexagram—the second and fifth lines. Traditionally, the second line is associated with the concept "subordinate" and the fifth line with that of "superior" or "ruler." In both cases, then, we have a representation of the ideal situation in which a yielding, or receptive line and an assertive, or creative line finds its counterpart in precisely the right location. Both hexagrams therefore symbolize the ideal relationship of wise ruler paired with a sage advisor, but in two different aspects.

That is not all, however, because the two hexagrams are also mirror images of each other, denoted by the term *zong*. [Figure 6.1] Deriving from the craft of weaving, this term originally referred to the tying of the longitudinal threads to the harnesses that alternately raise and lower the warp threads in different configurations to create the patterns in the weave. What this means in the case of *Tong ren* and *Da you* is that the one is immanent in the other, the one simultaneously *is* the other. Through the dynamics of their unique relationship the *Yin* line in the second place in "Fellowship with Men" advances to the ruling place in "Possession in Great Measure." In terms of the *Changes*, therefore, in a very real sense, "Possession in Great Measure" is immanent in "Fellowship with Men." Though portrayed graphically in linear fashion, and elaborated sequentially, in reality the elements and number symbolism of the one are the mirror image of the other.

In his prose poem Dong Zhongshu expressed this dynamic relationship linguistically by linking the two emblematic hexagrams by means of the coordinating conjunction *er*, thereby displaying the reciprocal dynamics embodied in the two hexagrams by means of a linear *verbal* representation. In this way Dong was able to convey immanence and complementarity syntactically. In other words, implicit in achieving "Fellowship with Men" is the realization of "Possession in Great Measure," which here refers to ascendancy to rulership of the empire. The "yielding" virtue of the superior man in a subordinate position rises to occupy the central and ruling place by virtue of his ability to expand the principles of Fellowship from the few to the many. In the language of the commentary, "the yielding finds its place, finds the middle, and the Creative corresponds with it; this means Fellowship with Men. . . . Only the superior man is able to unite the wills of all under heaven" (Wilhelm 1981:452).

The term *zong* for the mirror-image relationship between the two hexagrams "Unifying Men" and "Possession in Great Measure," like many of the most important metaphors in ancient Chinese philosophy relating to time and order, is drawn from cordage and the art of weaving. Other terms include *ji gang* ("fixed positions and motions with regard to other things in the web of Nature's relationships") (Needham and Wang 1956:555). This term is made up of *ji* ("leading thread, put in order" and by extension "keep time, chronicle of years, annals, period of years, 12-year cycle"); and *gang* ("cord forming the selvedge of a net; regulate; maintain in order; direct"). More concretely, the two terms are suggestive of an ancient record-keeping device structured like the Inka *quippu* which was said to have preceded the invention of writing in China. Defining *ji* as it applies to time, Michael Loewe stresses a linear view: "the term *chi*, or thread, suggests the line that is formed by a series of successive incidents or segments" (Loewe 1995:312). However, *ji* is equally frequently used to refer to constant periodicities such as those of the planets, especially Jupiter, or basic recurring cycles in calendrical calculations.

By far the most important of these terms from the weaver's craft are *ching* and *wei*. *Jing* is "the warp of a piece of woven goods," by extension "constant, order-giving principles; canonical text," and in our own day "meridian of longitude." *Wei* in contrast, are the "weft threads of a piece of woven goods," "the visible planets" which shuttle back and forth across the sky in opposition to the apparent east to west motion of the stars, "apocryphal, unorthodox commentaries on the Confucian canon," and in modern times "parallel of latitude." In the present context, *zong* is evocative of a *fabric of relationships*, made up of warp and weft, *sequentially linear though recursive in the making* (not unlike the hexagrams themselves and the numerical manipulations employed to derive them), but whose full composition and import can only be grasped in the totality of their complex patterning. The fabric of relations and philosophical ideals evoked exhibits a complementarity of principle and pattern, any segment of which is capable of invoking the whole tapestry. Again, it is not that the two hexagrams are linked as *cause and effect*, or that one brings the other into being. Rather, the one is simultaneously the other like the front and back of silk brocade.

With this in mind, consider the following explanation of dynastic prosperity and decline by the late Han scholar and iconoclast Wang Chong: "When the mandate of heaven [*tian ming*] is about to be launched, and a Sage-King is on the point of emerging, the material forces (*qi*), *before and after the event*, give proofs which will be radiantly manifest" (Hsiao 1979:594). Compare this with Dong Zhongshu's view a century and a half earlier: "Your servant has heard that in heaven's great conferring of responsibilities on the king there is something that human powers of themselves could not achieve, but that comes of itself. This is the sign that the Mandate [*ming*] has been granted. The people of the empire with one heart all turn to him as they would turn to their fathers and mothers. Thus it is that heaven's auspicious signs respond to [the people's] sincerity and come forth." Even in Wang Chong's time, the principle of causality invoked here in relation to auspicious portents tended to be understood simplistically by "mere prognosticators" in terms of cause and effect: "The errors of the School of Prognosticators are not in acknowledging the occurrences of calamities and auspicious happenings, but lie in their erroneous belief that the successes and failings of government bear a cause and effect relationship to those."

According to Wang, however,

> The accession of a worthy ruler happens to occur in an age that is going to be well governed; his virtues are self-evident above, and the people are automatically good below. The world is at peace and the people are secure. Auspicious signs all display themselves and the age speaks of those as induced by the worthy ruler. The immoral ruler happens to be born at a time when chaos is to exist; the empire is thrown into

troubles and the people's ways become disorderly, with unending disasters and calamities, leading to the fall of the state, the death of the ruler, and the displacement of his successors. The world all refers to that as having been induced by his evils. Such observations are clear about the external appearance of good and evil, but fail to perceive the internal reality of good and bad fortune. (Hsiao 1979:594)

In this view all the actions of an individual or an undertaking which is about to flourish will spontaneously accord with the timely factors of fate or *ming* (same term as *ming* "mandate" above). In the case of an emerging Sage King: "Followers will come to him unsummoned, and auspicious objects will come to him unsignaled. Invisibly moved, they will all arrive in concert as if sent" (Hsiao 1979:595). This is what Granet was referring to when he spoke of "patterns simultaneously appearing in a vast field of force," and Jung (1969) too, who stressed that the Chinese world-outlook involved a causality principle quite unlike that of Galilean-Newtonian science, which he denoted "synchronistic."

In linguistic terms, classical Chinese is tenseless, so temporal relations are somewhat fluid and typically marked contextually by the use of aspect particles and explicit time words. Indeed, aspect is one of the most difficult features of Chinese for the non-native speaker to master. Taken together, the two factors seem to militate in favor of a relative devaluation of precision when it comes to temporal indications, in favor of relational or situational content. This characteristic, like the account of the aged commoner at the feast, and Clifford Geertz's remark about "what kind of time it is" in Bali, brings to mind another suggestive parallel from the anthropological literature, an account of the cognitive devaluation of linear time among the Trobriand islanders first documented by Jacob Malinowski. Consider the following description of Trobriand concepts of time and temporality:

There is no boundary between past Trobriand experience and the present; he can indicate that an action is completed, but this does not mean that the action is past; it may be completed and present or timeless. Where we would say "Many years ago" and use the past tense, the Trobriander would say, "In my father's childhood" and use non-temporal verbs; he places the event situationally, not temporally. Past, present, and future are presented linguistically as the same, are present in his existence, and sameness with what we call the past and with myth, represents value to the Trobriander. . . . Temporality is meaningless . . . no tenses, no linguistic distinction between past or present. . . no arrangement of activities or events into means and ends, no causal or teleologic relationships. What we consider a causal relationship in a sequence of connected events, is to the Trobriander an ingredient of a patterned whole. . . .
There is organization or rather coherence in their acts because Trobriand activity is patterned activity. One act within this pattern brings into existence a pre-ordained cluster of acts. Perhaps one might find a parallel in our culture in the making of a sweater. When I embark on knitting one, the ribbing at the bottom does not *cause* the making of the neckline, nor of the sleeves or the armholes; and it is not part of a lineal series of acts. Rather it is an indispensable part of a patterned activity which includes all these other acts. . . . Trobriand islanders experience reality in nonlinear pattern because this is the valued reality. (Lee 1979:132, 135–36)

While the Trobriand islands are not China, one cannot help but be struck by the anthropologist's account of the Trobriander's valuation of a particular kind of reality and the homely knitting analogy. Perhaps in this description of the cultural devaluation of temporally structured narrative in favor of patterned relations and activity, we can gain an inkling of the cultural predisposition that prefigured the Chinese metaphorical recourse to the art of weaving. To the extent this is so, the early Chinese synthesis of the complementary aspects of time into an all-embracing fabric of acausal, patterned orderedness, far from being a metaphysical innovation of the immediate pre-imperial period, like many down-to-earth images in the *Book of Changes*, owes much to conceptual predispositions that hark back to China's archaic past.

References

Bodde, Derk. *Chinese Thought, Society, and Science: The Intellectual and Social Background of Science and Technology in Pre-modern China*. Honolulu, HI: University of Hawaii Press, 1991, 122–33.

Davies, Paul. "That Mysterious Flow." *Scientific American* 287, 3 (September 2002):42.

Fagg, Lawrence W. *Two Faces of Time*. Wheaton, IL: Theosophical Publishing House, 1985.

Hsiao, Kung-chuan. *History of Chinese Political Thought*, trans. F. W. Mote. Princeton, NJ: Princeton University Press, 1979.

Huang, Chun-Chieh, and Erik Zürcher, eds., *Time and Space in Chinese Culture*. Leiden: Brill, 1995.

Jung, C. G. "Synchronicity: an Acausal Connecting Principle." In *Collected Works of C. G. Jung, 2nd ed. Vol. 8: The Structure and Dynamics of the Psyche*. Princeton, NJ: Princeton University Press, 1969.

Lee, Dorothy. "Codifications of Reality: Lineal and Nonlineal." In R. E. Ornstein, ed., *The Nature of Human Consciousness*. San Francisco, CA: Freemann, 1973, 128–42.

Legge, James. *Zuo zhuan*. London: Trubner, 1861–72.

Lin, Li-chen. "The Concepts of Time and Position in the Book of Change and their Development." In Chun-Chieh Huang and Erik Zürcher, eds., *Time and Space in Chinese Culture*. Leiden: Brill, 1995, 89–113.

Loewe, Michael. "The Cycle of Cathay: Concepts of Time in Han China and their Problems." In Chun-Chieh Huang and Erik Zürcher, eds., *Time and Space in Chinese Culture*. Leiden: Brill, 1995, 305–28.

Keightley, David. *The Ancestral Landscape: Time, Space, and Community in Late Shang China (ca. 1200–1045 B.C.)*. Berkeley, CA: Institute of East Asian Studies, 2000.

Needham, Joseph. "Time and Knowledge in China and the West." In J. T. Fraser, ed., *The Voices of Time: A Cooperative Survey of Man's Views of Time as Expressed by the Sciences and by the Humanities* 2nd ed. Amherst, MA: University of Massachusetts Press, 1981, 133.

Needham, Joseph, and Wang Ling. *Science and Civilisation in China 2. History of Scientific Thought*. Cambridge: Cambridge University Press, 1956.

Nienhauser, W. H., ed. *The Grand Scribe's Records 1. The Basic Annals of Pre-Han China*. Bloomington, IN: Indiana University Press, 1994.

Pankenier, David W. "The Scholar's Frustration Reconsidered: Melancholia or Credo?" *Journal of the American Oriental Society* 110, 3 (1990):440.

Sima Qian. *Shiji*. Beijing: Zhonghua shuju, 1959.

Sivin, Nathan. "Chinese Conceptions of Time." *Earlham Review* 1 (1966):82–92.

Wilhelm, Richard. *The I Ching or Book of Changes*, rendered into English by Cary F. Baynes. Princeton, NJ: Princeton University Press, 1981.

7

TOPOGRAPHIES OF TIME
IN HESIOD

Alex Purves

In the late 8th century BCE, two poems attributed to the Greek poet Hesiod approached the structure and order of time from two different points of view. In the *Theogony*, an epic poem describing the evolution of the cosmos, Hesiod presents time as a linear construct, plotted upon a genealogical, diachronic history that runs from the birth of the gods to the present order of the universe. In the *Works and Days*, a didactic poem that instructs the reader on the correct way to manage a farm and a household, the poet focuses on the circular motion of time, as it is relayed through the cyclical pattern of seasons, months, and days. The two different temporalities that these poems engage in are in large part prescribed by their marked difference in genre; epic time will necessarily run according to a different logic than didactic, just as historical time will flow at a different rate to seasonal time (Strohm 2000:80–96; Koselleck 1985; Nowotny 1994). But while the temporalities of the two poems are largely separate, they also converge to offer new insights on, and new approaches to, the Hesiodic conception and construction of time.

This chapter will be mostly concerned with explicating the organization of time in the *Theogony*, but will begin by considering how the *Works and Days* sets certain prescriptions for time that may guide us in our reading of Hesiod in general. In both works, we shall seek to uncover the ways in which Hesiod contrives to hold time in abeyance through the domestic or agrarian metaphor of preserving goods in jars beneath the earth. Ultimately, this will lead to an argument for a spatial understanding of time in the *Theogony*, in which different temporal registers, such as the future and the past, are "stored" underground. By reading the time of the *Theogony*'s plot according to a topography of multiple dimensions, moreover, this paper aims to recover that sense of depth-within-time which scholars such as Erich Auerbach have sought to deny for ancient Greek epic.

Much of the *Works and Days* is concerned with training the farmer to recognize the correct times at which to carry out particular jobs (Leclerc 1994). Often these signs will point to times within a season or year (when the Sirius star begins to wane by day, start the wood-cutting—*Works and Days* 417–22; when the first crane flies overhead on its winter migration, fatten up the oxen for the fields—*Works and Days* 448–52). Toward the end of the poem there is also a section on the suitability of different days of the month for different events. The 12th day is good for a woman to set up her weaving, for example, the 4th propitious for marriage, the 13th bad for sowing crops (*Works and Days* 779, 800, 780–81). The *Works and Days* can thus be regarded as an elaborate set of instructions on how to seize the present moment, for each event—as a ὥριον ἔργον, or seasonal task—has its own precise point of timeliness within the ordered scheme of the Hesiodic calendar (641–42, 392ff., 422, 616–17, 697).

But this impulse toward grasping the ever-fleeting immediacy of the "right time" is countered by a more general thread that runs the poem, and that is the need to constantly live not in the present, but rather just one step ahead of it.

Figure 7.1 Early Iron Age pithos base in situ, pithos 2, TR61/62, Torone Chalkidike, courtesy of the Australian Archaeological Institute at Athens, Sydney, Australia.

Figure 7.2 Early Iron Age pithos 2 restored, courtesy of the Australian Archaeological Institute at Athens, Sydney, Australia.

Figure 7.3 Early Iron Age pithos base in situ, TR74, Torone Chalkidike, courtesy of the Australian Archaeological Institute at Athens, Sydney, Australia.

Throughout the *Works and Days*, Hesiod urges his audience to look forward consistently to, and to provide for, the unforeseeable future. There is a need, in other words, to ration out the present—to spread it thin over the less productive seasons of the year. The poet recommends doing this by storing up grain and wine in large jars (called variously πίθοι and ἄγγεα), which—along with a well-stocked granary—should only be broken open at certain specified times (cf. *Works and Days* 30–32, 93, 306–307, 361–63, 368–69, 411–12, 475, 498–504, 819). During his account of the threshing season, the poet advises the farmer to "transfer your grain into jars, using a measuring scoop/ Then store all your livelihood up and lock it in the house" (*Works and Days* 600–601), just as, during the vintage season, he calls for the farmer to draw wine into jars [εἰς ἄγγε᾽ ἀφύσαι] and preserve it for a later date (*Works and Days* 613–14).

Through the simple, everyday mechanism of the jar, Hesiod takes steps toward dividing time into the separate categories of past, present, and future. Its space thus serves as a "holding bay" for the present, or for the present-as-yet-unspent, a kind of container of time. This is not unlike Salman Rushdie's comparison of time to chutney in *Midnight's Children* (1980), whose narrator cooks pickles by day and writes history by night. As he puts it: "by day amongst the pickle-vats, by night within these sheets, I spend my time at the great work of preserving. Memory, as well as fruit, is being saved from the corruption of the clocks" (38). Hesiod too, in his book about the management not of history but of the continuous cycle of the year, comments on the practice of "archiving"—of preserving what in the present will soon be "past" for a new time in the future.

In his narration of the story of Pandora, near the beginning of the *Works and Days*, Hesiod expands upon the temporal significance of the jar. For it is in opening the *pithos* given to her by Zeus that Pandora creates a new space in time, what Hesiod elsewhere calls the "iron age" of men:

πρὶν μὲν γὰρ ζώεσκον ἐπὶ χθονὶ φῦλ' ἀνθρώπων   90
νόσφιν ἄτερ τε κακῶν καὶ ἄτερ χαλεποῖο πόνοιο
νούσων τ' ἀργαλέων αἵ τ' ἀνδράσι κῆρας ἔδωκαν·   92
ἀλλὰ γυνὴ χείρεσσι πίθου μέγα πῶμ' ἀφελοῦσα   94
ἐσκέδασ'· ἀνθρώποισι δ' ἐμήσατο κήδεα λυγρά.   95
μούνη δ' αὐτόθι Ἐλπὶς ἐν ἀρρήκτοισι δόμοισιν
ἔνδον ἔμιμνε πίθου ὑπὸ χείλεσιν, οὐδὲ θύραζε
ἐξέπτη· πρόσθεν γὰρ ἐπέμβαλε πῶμα πίθοιο
αἰγιόχου βουλῇσι Διὸς νεφεληγερέταο.

[For before that time, the race of men who lived upon the earth
Were far from evils, grievous toil,
And the baneful diseases which bring death to men.
But the woman removed the great lid of the jar with her hands,
Scattering them all. And she brought hard sorrows to mankind.
Hope alone remained there in its well-built house,
It stayed inside the jar, beneath the lip, nor did it fly outside
Before she put the lid of the jar back on,
By the plan of aegis-bearing, cloud-gathering Zeus.]
(*Works and Days* 90–99)

Between πρίν and πρόσθεν (both words meaning "before"), Pandora opens up a new region in time as she opens up the space of the jar. For, in the gap between these two temporal adverbs, the race of iron is created (*Works and Days* 174ff), forever caught in the cycle of mortal birth and death which hovers in the brief period between the opening and shutting of the jar. It is not only disease and sorrows that Pandora allows to escape by lifting the lid of her *pithos*, but time as well, resigning humans to a fate trapped between the hedges of the past and future, in a present which is to be spent and re-spent in a continuous cycle.

For the generation that Pandora creates, the ability to see beyond the present will forever be blinded by forgetfulness (see Detienne 1996:85–86; Nagy 1992; Thalmann 1984:147–48; Walsh 1984:22–36;

Pucci 1977:22–27; Cole 1983;Vernant 1983), in one direction, and hope in the other, two factors that, for Hesiod, symbolize the mortal condition, or "iron age" (*Works and Days* 986–87; Pucci 1977:103–105). It is hope alone that remains for humans, trapped within the rim of Pandora's jar.

Hesiod's insistent reminder to preserve for the future thus reads as a corrective to Pandora's act, by ensuring that the lid of the farmer's jar is not opened before its time: "open a jar on the fourth day" (*Works and Days* 819–20), "Satisfy yourself from the jar at the beginning and end / But hold off in the middle" (368–69), "So the ripe ears of corn may nod towards the ground/ If Olympian Zeus should grant you such a fortunate outcome in the future/ And then you may brush the cobwebs from your storage jars" (473–75). As Hesiod explains it, hope is a deceptive means of providing for the future, because it obscures the crucial difference between that which still is (ἔτι) and that which always is (αἰεί):

ἐλπὶς δ᾽ οὐκ ἀγαθὴ κεχρημένον ἄνδρα κομίζειν
ἥμενον ἐν λέσχῃ, τῷ μὴ βίος ἄρκιος εἴη.
δείκνυε δὲ δμώεσσι θέρεος ἔτι μέσσου ἐόντος·
"οὐκ αἰεὶ θέρος ἐσσεῖται· ποιεῖσθε καλιάς."

[Hope is not good at providing for a needy man,
Idling in the lounge, when his livelihood is not secure.
Point out to your workers when it is still [ἔτι] the middle of summer,
"It will not always αἰεὶ be summer. Build your granaries!"]
(*Works and Days* 500–503)

Hesiod's use of granaries, store houses, and jars as mechanisms for regulating time in the *Works and Days* speaks to a human attempt to outdo, or at least—by explicitly reversing Pandora's act—to undo, the limited temporal horizons of mortals in the age of iron. In the *Theogony*, it is possible to push this concept of "stored time" further and, in so doing, to uncover some of the central problems that the modern critic has faced in his approach to epic time.

The *Theogony* deals not with the limited range of human time, but rather with the expansive and conflicting temporalities of divine mythology. Hesiod's history of the cosmos begins with the emergence of the earth, Gaia, from the undefined matter of Chaos. Gaia then partners with the sky (Ouranos). Ouranos, however, attempts to block the release of Gaia's progeny by continually covering her in the act of intercourse, until his son, Kronos, castrates him from inside his mother's womb. At this point, Ouranos is deposed and Kronos marries his sister, Rhea. Again, though, in an attempt to ward off the succession of future children, Kronos swallows each of his offspring as soon as they are born. Zeus, the last child, survives because his mother hides him in a cave and tricks Kronos into consuming a stone instead. He too thereby deposes his father, but here the diachronic sequence of history stops. For Zeus successfully swallows his pregnant wife, Metis, and gives birth to the virgin Athena through his head, thus bringing the line of female procreation (and filial succession) to an end.

The central problem of the *Theogony* lies in reconciling this diachronic genealogy of the gods with the synchronic, eternal present ushered in by Zeus, who alone of the immortals manages successfully to put a halt to the progression of time. For Zeus not only overcomes the older gods of the past, but he also, by swallowing both offspring and wife, transforms his own body into a container that holds the future indefinitely in reserve.

How, then, do the categories of the past and the future fit within a divine time scheme where that which is "always" (αἰεί/αἰέν) stretches elastically from one end of Zeus' rule to the other? Furthermore, how do we reconcile Zeus and the race of gods who are repeatedly described as those "who always are" with the human temporalities of birth, death, and narrative? Hesiod acknowledges the problem at the very beginning of the *Theogony*, in his account of the initiation he first received from the Muses on Mount Helicon:

> ἐνέπνευσαν δέ μοι αὐδὴν
> θέσπιν, ἵνα κλείοιμι τά τ' ἐσσόμενα πρό τ' ἐόντα,
> καί μ' ἐκέλονθ' ὑμνεῖν μακάρων γένος αἰὲν ἐόντων,
> σφᾶς δ' αὐτὰς πρῶτόν τε καὶ ὕστατον αἰὲν ἀείδειν.

[They breathed into me a divine voice,
In order that I might celebrate *the things of the future and the past*
And they bid me to hymn the race of the gods *who always (αἰέν) are*
But to sing *always* (αἰέν) of themselves *both first and last*.]
(*Theogony* 31–34)

The emphasis in these lines on the voice and its ability to tell a story draws attention to the role of narrative in framing the discordance between the unbroken timeline signaled by αἰέν, on the one hand, and the division of time into a temporal sequence ("the things of the future and the past"; "first and last") on the other. The Muses confront Hesiod with two different versions of time at once—one which is static and all-encompassing, the other which travels like an arrow from the past to the future. But what exactly do the Muses mean when they instruct Hesiod to sing of the "future" and the "past" in this context? Although they acknowledge that narrative must always be organized into a temporal frame that runs in sequence from "first" to "last," the Muses also present Hesiod with a time span within which the categories of past and future should technically no longer have a place, since they have been consumed and flattened out into the eternal "now" of Zeus' rule.

It is precisely this concept of a unilateral, all-pervasive present that Eric Auerbach argued constituted the primary characteristic of archaic Greek epic. In his famous reading of Odysseus's scar, Auerbach (1953) insisted that every scene in Homer "knows only a foreground, only a uniformly illuminated, uniformly objective present" (7). He consistently uses terms such as "illumination," "clear," "light," and "visible" to describe the effects of this epic present, and his reading excludes, quite forcefully, all hints of the shadow or depth that emerge from what he calls "the darkness of the past": "Homer will not [let Odysseus's scar] appear out of the darkness of an unilluminated past; it must be set in full light. . . Never is there a form left fragmentary or half-illuminated, never a lacuna, never a gap, never a glimpse of unplumbed depths" (6–7).

A similar resistance to the spatial "layering" of time can be found in the work of the Polish Classicist Thaddaeus Zielinski, whose treatment of plot in ancient epic is founded upon the concept of events stretched out upon a single, two-dimensional plane. In 1901, Zielinski formulated a law, still generally accepted today, that Greek epic never presents two events as if they occurred simultaneously. Rather than traversing the same temporal space twice, archaic epic instead conceives of simultaneous actions consecutively, as if they occurred one after the other. By eliminating the concept of "meanwhile" from the Homeric lexicon, Zielinski's theory refutes the possibility of epic time occupying transverse or "horizontal" space (a conception of time that has since been explored by scholars such as Benjamin 1968:261 and Anderson 1991:22-31). He based his findings on what he termed the eye's inability to apprehend multiple dimensions of time and space at once: "So ist mein Sehn aus einem dreiplanigen plötzlich ein einplaniges geworden: die neu hinzugetretene Dimension der Zeit hat die Raumdimension der Tiefe verdrängt" [Thus my vision suddenly becomes one-dimensional from three: the newly-added dimension of time has replaced the spatial dimension of depth] (Zielinski 1901:409).

Like Auerbach, Zielinski proposes that there is no "depth" to time. This provides the basis for his larger claim that poetry, like aesthetics, cannot conceive of the simultaneous events of a plot in parallel space (Zielinski 1901:414). By focusing so exclusively on the singularity of the present, Zielinski paved the way for other scholars of his generation and after, such as Fränkel (1968) and Page (1955), who argued that in archaic epic, time had no three-dimensionality, or sense of a proportionate whole, but was rather organized as a disjointed amalgam of events which bore hardly any intrinsic relation to each other (in the wake of early scholars like Zielinski and Auerbach, see the important work of Austin 1966; Krischer 1971; Frazer 1981; Whitman and Scodel 1981; Lynn-George 1988; Olson 1995:91–119).

Although critics of epic time pay little attention to Hesiod, they do include him in their stipulations. Zielinski's law, for example, has been applied equally to the *Theogony* as it has to the *Iliad* and *Odyssey*. The complexity of time zones in Hesiod's poem poses an interesting problem, however, for the *Theogony*—on the level of narrative content at least—does combine two different registers of time (mortal and immortal, or sequential and eternal) simultaneously. As West's commentary notes, Hesiod breaks Zielinski's law on two occasions in the *Theogony*, and both of these transgressions occur, crucially, at the point when Zeus is attempting to effect the transition from diachronic to synchronic time; that is, at the beginning and end of his battle with the Titans, the decisive conflict that establishes his rule for eternity (West 1966:617, 711; Frazer 1981).

In order to win the Titanomachy, Zeus must gain the assistance of a group of ancient immortals known as the Hundred Handers, who had long ago been imprisoned underground by their father Ouranos:

Ὀβριάρεῳ δ' ὡς πρῶτα πατὴρ ὠδύσσατο θυμῷ
Κόττῳ τ' ἠδὲ Γύγῃ, δῆσε κρατερῷ ἐνὶ δεσμῷ,
ἠνορέην ὑπέροπλον ἀγώμενος ἠδὲ καὶ εἶδος
καὶ μέγεθος· κατένασσε δ' ὑπὸ χθονὸς εὐρυοδείης.
ἔνθ' οἵ γ' ἄλγε' ἔχοντες ὑπὸ χθονὶ ναιετάοντες
εἴατ' ἐπ' ἐσχατιῇ μεγάλης ἐν πείρασι γαίης
δηθὰ μάλ' ἀχνύμενοι, κραδίῃ μέγα πένθος ἔχοντες.
ἀλλά σφεας Κρονίδης τε καὶ ἀθάνατοι θεοὶ ἄλλοι
οὓς τέκεν ἠύκομος Ῥείη Κρόνου ἐν φιλότητι
Γαίης φραδμοσύνῃσιν ἀνήγαγον ἐς φάος αὖτις·

When their father (Ouranos) first grew angry at Obriareos,
Kottos and Gyges, he bound them in strong chains,
In awe of their overbearing strength and appearance
And size, and *settled them under the wide-paved earth*.
There under the earth they lived in grievance
Lurking at the furthermost limits on the edges of the great earth,
Sorely distressed, and harbouring great sorrow in their hearts.
But Zeus and the other immortal gods
Whom Rhea bore in partnership with Kronos
Brought them up into the light again under the advice of Gaia.
(*Theogony* 617–26)

At the same time as Zeus reaches under the earth to retrieve the Hundred Handers, the *Theogony*'s narrative also steps back to an earlier moment in time within the body of the story, to a point during the rule of Ouranos ("when first . . ."), thus crossing the same temporal space twice. There is a "meanwhile," then, in Hesiod's narrative, but it is confined to the space of underground, where the ancient gods wait until it is their time to reappear. In breach of Zielinski's law, the *Theogony* houses a different register of time under the earth, which runs independently of the time upon its surface. At line 626, these two temporal threads are reunited into a single narrative plane, as the Hundred Handers are brought "into the light again" from the "depths of the past," and re-integrated with the present.

The space beneath the earth thereby serves as a kind of narrative repository within which the plot "stores up" time for the future, in much the same way as Hesiod, in the *Works and Days*, advises his brother to store up and preserve the time of the present in large jars that were sunk underground. Even Pandora, who otherwise lets the contents of her jar escape, is able to at least store up hope for future time inside her *pithos*.

Hesiod thus uses underground space to "archive" time, in precisely the way that Auerbach and Zielinski sought to deny for epic poetry. I borrow the analogy of the archive from a medieval scholar,

Paul Strohm (2000), who in turn adapts it from Derrida's *Archive Fever* (1996). In Strohm's words, "the archive does not arrest time, but rather exists as an unstable amalgam of unexhausted past and unaccomplished future" (80). In the immortal setting of Hesiod's *Theogony*, the past is always unexhausted. Since the gods cannot pass out of existence, so too can the past never be brought to full completion. It can only be removed from the present by being contained or put on hold for some moment in the future.

When Ouranos traps Gaia's children within her subterranean belly, therefore, he plays on the common analogy between womb and jar in Greek thought (Dean-Jones 1994:65) by utilizing her belly as a storage space within which he hopes to hold back the onset of the plot's chronological sequence, just as his "binding" of the Hundred Handers and imprisonment of them under the earth may be understood, metaphorically, as a "binding" of narrative time (Brooks 1984:101). Furthermore, Christopher Faraone (1992) has shown how the techniques of both binding and burial were commonly practiced in apotropaic ritual precisely in order to avert or ward off some future event. By binding an image of a god, or by sealing an image or token within a pot and burying it, the actant sought to exert his own control over time; to manipulate the approach of the future or to temporarily arrest time within the present. "The Geoponica (10.87.6) recommends attaching verse 5.387 of the Ares passage ('and three months and ten he lay chained in a bronze cauldron') to a tree to prevent it from prematurely casting its fruit—that is, it 'binds' the tree to hold on to its fruit until the correct moment in its annual cycle" (Faraone 1992:286).

In Homer, Odysseus nearly transcends the long passage of time which separates him from Ithaca, thanks to the temporary binding of the winds by Aeolus. In the *Iliad*, on the other hand, we are told of how Ares once lay bound in strong chains for thirteen months in a bronze jar, and almost perished as a result (5.384–91)—a testimony to the considerable power that binding and entombment can exert over even the immortals' control over time.

As the *Theogony* moves forward to the "everlasting present" of Zeus' reign, therefore, it is also restrained by a narrative movement which seeks to bind time within a space which—as the story progresses—will come to symbolize the "depths of the past." The exit of the Hundred Handers from the dark regions underground (*Theogony* 617–26) is thus a narratological move as well as a spatial one, as the text retraces its steps into the archive of its past in order to return certain key elements of the plot to the light of the present.

We have seen how Auerbach used binaries of light and darkness to describe the difference between the present (visible, illuminated, and surface) and the future or the past (dark, murky, and subterranean). It is here that we can draw the clearest analogy between his understanding of epic time and Hesiod's temporal landscape. For throughout the *Theogony*, the present is represented as that which is visible, while the past and the future linger under the cover of darkness or ground. The dark, subterranean cavern has long been used as refuge or hide-out from chronological time. Epimenides, who—legend has it—fell asleep in a cave, slipped out of time for a period of 57 years (Diels-Kranz fr. 3, Dodds 1951:207–35). Similarly, Ouranos attempts to indefinitely "hide" the future by forcing his offspring to remain underground:

πάντας ἀποκρὲς φάος οὐκ ἀνίεσκε
Γαίης ἐν κευθμῶνι

[[Ouranos] would not let them come up into the light, but hid them all Within the passages of the earth.] (*Theogony* 157–58)

The *Theogony*, then, charts the development of time in three dimensions, complete with pockets and dwellings within which the past and the future can recede. When the infant Zeus is hidden within a subterranean cave (*Theogony* 482–3) until he grows strong enough to wrest power from his father, or when we are told that Zeus's thunderbolt had previously (τὸ πρίν) been hidden beneath the earth (*Theogony* 505), as if being saved up for its crucial role at a later point in the story, we come to understand that another level of temporality exists below the surface of the ever-visible present of eternal, immortal time.

In contrast to Auerbach's formulation for the *Odyssey*, however, within which he stated that "Homeric style knows only a foreground, only a uniformly illuminated, uniformly objective present" (7), in Hesiod the "depths of the past" cast a considerable shadow over narrative movement, as if to suppress and all but overwhelm the emergence of the present. Ouranos's restraining of his children within the belly of Gaia serves to indefinitely postpone the transition into the future, just as Kronos's own swallowing of his children attempts to put a hold on the passage of time.

The *Theogony* is balanced by a pair of conflicting impulses: the impulse to move forward in time, following the linear progression of language, genealogy, and history, and the impulse to suspend time, to restrain it within a dilatory space which, instead of sending time forward, pulls it back into the past. The poem has reckoned with this tension from the very beginning, as it has been played out in the plot's movement from matrilineal to patrilineal descent, and from diachronic to synchronic time (see Arthur 1982 for further binary recasting). As Zeus attempts to close the gap between these two poles, he is left with the need for a place where his own troubling history, as manifested by the paradoxically ancient-but-ageless Titans (πρότεροι θεοί, *Theogony* 424, 486), can be disposed of.

Hesiod solves the problem by creating a place within the text where those temporalities may be contained. We have already seen that Hesiod uses the space underground as a kind of archive, or jar, within which he could store up narrative elements for the future. In terms of the stratification of time in his poem, we have seen how the earth provides Hesiod with a second layer of temporal space which runs in parallel to the surface narrative, although often at a different rate. This is no less true for his description of Tartaros, a region sunk deep beneath the earth with a geography and chronology of its own. For Hesiod, Tartaros functions as that place in the text where the narrative may resolve the complexities of its own transferal from one perception of time to another and within which it may even confine these complexities, in much the same way as Zeus uses it as a space to restrain and confine the Titans.

Located as far underground as it takes for an anvil to fall for nine days, Tartaros is encircled by an impenetrable wall of bronze, three layers of darkness, and the backward-flowing streams of the river Ocean. In keeping with its circular and static geography, Hesiod describes Tartaros in language that cycles through a series of repetitions which either follow too closely upon one another (*Theogony* 722–5) or, atypically for the poet (Sellschopp 1967), replay without variation (736–9 = 807–10). Both narratologically and topographically, therefore, the underworld is a place without progress or development through time. Instead, it is bound by the laws of stasis and repetition. In some cases, as with the exchange of Night and Day across its threshold (*Theogony* 748–54), that repetition validates the cyclical, natural patterns of time in the world above. But for those trapped within the walls of Tartaros, there is explicitly no exit, no "place" for time to go (*Theogony* 732, 772). The Underworld is thus, in both cases, the site of repetition, but repetition without variation (Pucci 1997), without the movement forward or out which is a necessary prerequisite for all successful story-telling (Todorov 1977:233; Brooks 1984:90ff). In this way, the underworld draws together the "archive" of the space underground, where time is held back, with the dreadful state of repetition found at the edges of the earth, the place where Prometheus's liver, for example, is endlessly replicated. In each case, these extreme locales serve to trap or hide time at the edges of the narrative (Johnson 1999: 12–13).

In terms of the geography of plot, Tartaros thus serves as the site to which all dead ends lead—within which the machinery of various unfulfilled (but ever-present) story-lines winds down and is abandoned. Although Zeus cannot destroy his immortal forebears, he can stop their succession through narrative. By placing them within the sequestered space of Tartaros he creates a topographical equivalent of the "depths of the past" to which their mythic identity will always be bound.

As already observed, Zeus's actions in this case are similar to those of the Titans before him, who sought to fix the present in their own time by breaking the cycle of filial succession. Ouranos's entrapment of his children within Gaia's womb, like Kronos's entrapment of his children within his own belly, is analogous to Zeus's suppression of those who pose a threat to the permanence of his sovereignty and imprisonment of them within the belly of the Underworld. For, in order to reach Tartaros, one must first pass through a great chasm (740) which West (1966) links with the god Chaos, and suggests may be envisioned as a throat (116). That throat looks back to the throat of Kronos, and forward to Zeus's own swallowing of Metis later in the poem. It also opens up a space in the narrative which both West (1997:297) and Walcot (1961, 1966:61), drawing on Near Eastern parallels, have compared to a large metal jar.

By fashioning Tartaros as a kind of vast, makeshift jar that—unlike the jars of the *Works and Days*—will never be opened, Zeus definitively separates off the categories of the past and future from his own all-encompassing present. In the present analysis of the jar in the *Works and Days*, we saw how it worked as a kind of archive within which the past could be stored for the future. But the principal function of the archive is of course its role in preserving memory, of saving time from the disintegration of the past. In the immortal world of the *Theogony*, however, the underground storage space becomes a refuge, a means of artificially creating a past in a synchronic universe. For, if mortals use forgetfulness and hope to categorize that which is past and that which remains to take place in the future, then the Olympians—who can instantly see through both of these devices—are left with the problem of having nowhere to "put" their past or at least of setting it out of sight. In this sense Tartaros functions as an archive which binds a previous but ever-present generation of gods in an eternal state of stasis and repetition, as if "frozen" in an earlier age. More importantly, and also paradoxically, Tartaros functions as a kind of "oubliette," a secret underground dungeon, which (as its etymology suggests) substitutes for the human process of forgetting.

Jean-Pierre Vernant has described Hesiodic time as not a single, linear structure but as a "stratification of layers" (1983:36). We have attempted to expand on that metaphor here by thinking of time in the *Theogony* in terms of a topography, where the temporal discrepancies of the poem are externalized into spatial components. Rather than adhere to the concept forwarded by Zielinski and Auerbach, among others, that Greek epic narrative plays itself out in only two dimensions, the *Theogony* offers us a glimpse of a subterranean time that, despite Zeus's machinations, never entirely disappears beneath the surface of Hesiod's world.

References

Anderson, Benedict. *Imagined Communities*. London: Verso, 1991.

Arthur, Marilyn. "Cultural Strategies in Hesiod's *Theogony*: Law, Family, Society." *Arethusa* 15 (1982):63–81.

Auerbach, Erich. *Mimesis: The Representation of Reality in Western Literature*. Princeton, NJ: Princeton University Press, 1953.

Austin, Norman. "The Function of the Digression in the *Iliad*." *Greek, Roman, and Byzantine Studies* 7 (1966):295–312.

Benjamin, Walter. *Illuminations*. New York: Routledge, 1968.

Brooks, Peter. *Reading for the Plot: Design and Intention in Narrative*. New York: Alfred A. Knopf, 1984.

Cole, Thomas. "Archaic Truth." *Quaderni Urbinati di Cultura Classica* 13 (1983):7–28.

Dean-Jones, Lesley. *Women's Bodies in Classical Greek Science*. Oxford: Clarendon Press, 1994.

Derrida, Jacques. *Archive Fever*. Chicago, IL: University of Chicago Press, 1996.

Detienne, Marcel. *The Masters of Truth in Archaic Greece*. New York: Zone, 1996.

Diels, H., and W. Kranz, eds. *Die Fragmente der Vorsokratiker*. Berlin: Weidmann, 1951.

Dodds, E. R. *The Greeks and the Irrational*. Berkeley, CA: University of California Press, 1951.

Faraone, Christopher. *Talismans and Trojan Horses*. Oxford: Oxford University Press: 1992.

Fränkel, Hermann. *Wege und Formen Frühgriechischen Denkens*. Munich: 1968.

Frazer, R.M. "Hesiod's Titanomachy as an Illustration of Zielinski's Law." *Greek, Roman, and Byzantine Studies* 22.1 (1981):5–9.

Johnson, David M. "Hesiod's Description of Tartarus (*Theogony* 721-819)." *Phoenix* 53 (1999):8–28.

Koselleck, Reinhart. *Futures Past: On the Semantics of Historical Time*. Cambridge, MA: MIT Press, 1985.

Krischer, Tilman. *Formale Konventionen der homerischen Epik*. Munich: Beck, 1971.

Leclerc, Marie-Christine. "Facettes du Temps dans les *Travaux et les Jours* d'Hésiode." *Revue de Philologie* 68 (1994):147–63.

Lynn-George, Michael. *Epos: Word, Narrative and the Iliad*. Atlantic Highlands, NJ: Prometheus, 1988.

McLoughlin, Beatrice. "The Pithos Makers at Zagora, Andros in the 8th Century B.C." MA thesis. University of Sydney, 2000.

Nagy, Gregory. "Authorisation and Authorship in the Hesiodic *Theogony*." *Ramus* 21 (1992):119–30.

Nowotny, Helga. *Time: the Modern and Postmodern Experience*. Cambridge: Polity Press, 1994.

Olson, S. Douglas. *Blood and Iron: Stories and Storytelling in Homer's Odyssey*. Leiden: Brill, 1995.

Page, Denys. *The Homeric Odyssey*. Oxford: Oxford University Press, 1955.

Pucci, Pietro. *Hesiod and the Language of Poetry*. Baltimore, MD: Johns Hopkins University Press, 1977.

Rushdie, Salman. *Midnight's Children*. New York: Jonathan Cape, 1980.

Sellschopp, Inez. *Stilistische Untersuchungen zu Hesiod*. Darmstadt: Wissenschaftliche Buchgesellschaft, 1967.

Strohm, Paul. *Theory and the Premodern Text*. Minneapolis, MN: University of Minnesota Press, 2000.

Thalmann, William. *Conventions of Form and Thought in Early Greek Epic Poetry*. Baltimore, MD: Johns Hopkins University Press, 1984.

Todorov, Tzvetan. *The Poetics of Prose*. Ithaca, NY: Cornell University Press, 1977.

Vernant, Jean-Pierre. *Myth and Thought Among the Greeks*. Boston, MA: Routledge, 1983.

Walcot, Peter. *Hesiod and the Near East*. Cardiff: University of Wales Press, 1966.

———. "Pandora's Jar: *Erga* 83–105." *Hermes* 89 (1961):249–51.

Walsh, George. *The Varieties of Enchantment*. Chapel Hill, NC: University of North Carolina Press, 1984.

West, M. L. *The East Face of Helicon*. Oxford: Oxford University Press, 1997

———. *Hesiod: Theogony*. Oxford: Oxford University Press, 1966.

Whitman, Cedric, and Ruth Scodel. "Sequence and Simultaneity in *Iliad* N, Ζ, and O." *Harvard Studies in Classical Philology* 85 (1981):1–15.

Zielinski, Thaddeus. "Die Behandlung Gleichzeitiger Ereignisse im Antiken Epos." *Philologus* suppl. VIII, Heft 3, 1901.

8

GREEK CHRONOGRAPHIC TRADITIONS ABOUT THE FIRST OLYMPIC GAMES

Astrid Möller

The first Olympic Games are commonly believed to have occurred in the year 776 BCE. With this date, many have held, history begins in Greece, even in Europe. Some scholars, however, have cast doubt on the accuracy of this date, and it is no longer easy to believe that we actually have a fixed date in Greece from the 8th century BCE. During this time, the Greeks only started to write and had not yet created documents which would prove such a date. Considering the sanctuary at Olympia, the archaeological evidence suggests that the games began in the 7th century. Around 700 BCE, the area of the sanctuary was leveled, and shortly after this time wells were increasingly sunk into the ground, presumably to cater to the growing needs of athletes and visitors. Not until the 6th century do we find actual remains of a stadium (Mallwitz 1988, 1999; Sinn 1996).

Although our available material evidence actually argues against the traditional dating of the first Olympic Games to 776 BCE, this chronographical problem serves as an excellent example of the processes by which ancient Greek chronographers arrived at these dates in the first place, and it demonstrates clearly how deeply implicated ancient chronography was in various contemporary cultural and discursive traditions. It is perhaps somewhat ironic, therefore, as we shall see in the course of this chapter, that we have every reason to doubt the authenticity of the traditional foundation date of the Olympic Games, but little chance that we could ever find a better date which would be as precise.

Ancient chronography has two meanings in the context of classical historiography. On the one hand, it is a historiographical genre. Felix Jacoby (1909:88) held that it began with Hellanicus of Lesbos at the end of the 5th century BCE. During the Hellenistic Period it took the shape of chronological tables, even though we do not know when synchronistic tables actually started. It might have been with Castor of Rhodes in the 1st century BCE, although there is no direct evidence, or with Eusebius in the 4th century CE, whose chronicle was evidently organized in parallel columns. David Asheri (1991/92:54) argued for Timaeus of Tauromenium, who lived somewhere between 350 and 250 BCE, as the inventor of synchronistic tables. Chronography thus describes a record of historical events precisely dated by reference to an absolute chronological system. On the other hand, the term "chronography" is used to refer to the process in which precise dates were established for persons and events not yet included in an absolute chronology (Mosshammer 1979:85). This is the situation at the beginning of historiography in the 5th century BCE, when Greek historians started to establish ways to date events.

In a world without documents that already contain events dated by years of kings, magistrates, or other systems, historians had to find ways to date events. Ancient Greek scholars created a network of dates by drawing diachronic and synchronic lines, composing a temporal co-ordinate system similar to the spatial one used for geographical maps. In 1966, the Italian historian Santo Mazzarino argued against the schematic attribution of cyclical time perception to the Greeks and linear time perception to Judaeo-Christian thought (1966, 2.2: 412–61, n. 555). He held that the typical way to set up a chronology in classical historiography was what he called the diastematic system of dating.

The Greek word *diastema* means "interval," "difference," or "extension," "dimension"; *diastematikos* means proceeding in intervals, indicating distance or having dimension. According to Mazzarino, the backbone of classical chronology is made up by time intervals between more or less important events. In Greek chronology, each event had to be located in time in relation to other events which was expressed by intervals in years or generations and in synchronisms between them. Consequently, a network of synchronic and diachronic coordinate axes was created (Daffinà 1987). A major hindrance to chronology arose from the lack of a fixed point of reference, such as for example, the birth of Christ in Western civilization, from which point events are counted forward and backward (It was Dionysius Exiguus in the 6th century who fixed Christ's birth to 525 years before his own time. The calculation *ante Christum natum*, however, was only introduced by Dionysius Petavius who published his *Opus de Doctrina Temporum* in 1627). Instead, the Greeks had to build their chronology from within to locate each event at a certain distance to and from another.

Synchronic lines had to be found by creating synchronisms between persons, the foundation of cities, or famous battles. The ability to establish that two events occurred at the same time not only coordinated events but also provided the possibility of connecting two different dating systems which might have been current in two different cities.

Diachronic devices were provided to a certain extent by genealogies (see Möller 1996 for reservations) and by lists of eponymous magistrates, priestesses or victors. Genealogies naturally give only rough generations, and matters are made even more confusing by the fact that ancient authors often have different notions of what constitutes a "generation length" (Meyer 1892–99:151-88; Pearson 1942:9-12; Prakken 1943; den Boer 1954:5–29; van Compernolle

1959; Miller 1955, 1965, 1970, 1971). What is more, Greek genealogies mostly deal with mythical figures who are only very rarely explicitly connected to the historical present (Thomas 1989; Henige 1974). The lists of historical figures were not treated much differently. Genealogies could be transformed into king lists and vice versa, according to necessity. The manipulation of genealogies or lists became more urgent when synchronization of persons was required. We should not believe that this is a phenomenon occurring in oral societies. The concept of synchronizing generations itself requires written methods and probably a written mode of study.

Lists of eponymous magistrates are, however, more promising for accurate dating in giving an annual pattern for counting single years. Unfortunately, we do not have any evidence of such lists before 435–415 BCE, when the first archon-list was inscribed at Athens (see now Hedrick 2002). Likewise, it is important to emphasize that the later epigraphical lists we find from the Hellenistic period into Roman times had no significance in historiography, not even in local history as far as we can tell. Besides, they do not provide more information than the sequence of office-holders with an occasional comment. This is far from what we expect of a chronicle and does not give us the documents needed to date events. Not until a chronographer puts a name from a list and an event together can we consider a historical event to be dated.

Chronicles were uncommon in Greece, since the Greeks tended to prefer a narrative or literary history to the dry listing of annual magistrates and events, with the Marmor Parium seeming to be one of the very few exceptions. There is some evidence for an annalistic pattern in historiographical literature, but it followed far more the narrative conditions of Greek historiography than what we would find, for example, in Near Eastern or medieval chronicles. It seems that scholars writing local histories—if they used an annalistic pattern at all—did not find the material in archives, but had first to draw up a list of local kings, magistrates, or priests (Möller 2001).

Thus, early Greek chronography is not just a construction based on generation reckoning by means of genealogies, or the simple counting of annual magistrates, but a far more complex and comprehensive tradition (Mosshammer 1979:101-105). Apparently there is no abstract model of chronographic theory; it is the individual tradition which determines each date. In the words of Alden Mosshammer, "early Greek chronology is not a problem to be 'solved,' but a tradition to be understood and respected" (1979:86). In this sense, it is not helpful to simply change, knock down, or overturn ancient dates even if they seem entirely bogus. It is necessary, rather, to look for the processes by which they were created and passed on.

Much of Greek chronology since the 3rd century BCE is based on counting Olympiads. The Olympic games took place every fourth year, and the interval was counted as first, second, third, fourth year of Olympiad X. The list of the Olympic victors, which is the basis of this calculation, is said to have been edited by Hippias of Elis at the end of the 5th century BCE or perhaps a little later. Scholars have discussed Hippias' sources for more than a hundred years now and the question is still not settled. On the whole, one can distinguish between optimists who believe that Hippias found an official list in the temple archive at Olympia which he then published (Asheri 1991/92:53; Bengtson 1971:21; Finley and Pleket 1976:12), and pessimists or skeptics who declare Hippias to be a liar and forger who invented the names at least before the 6th century BCE (Mahaffy 1881; Körte 1904; Beloch 1929; Peiser 1990. Bilik 1996, 2000 for bibliography).

All arguments are built on poor evidence. To state it clearly: Of Hippias's *anagraphé* not a single fragment survived. Everything we try to establish about this work is therefore purely conjectural. The only testimony is given by Plutarch, who declared in *Numa* 1.6 that the list of the Olympic victors is said to have been published late by Hippias without a trustworthy basis for this work. Plutarch's negative assessment of Hippias's work is easier to understand in its context within his vita of Numa: It was most likely prompted by Plutarch's annoyance at the difficulties of dating Numa (Bultrighini 1990:206-7).

Neither Hippias's sources nor the shape of his work with the title *Olympionikon anagraphé* can be reconstructed. Other lost works with similar titles like *Olympionikai* or *Olympiades* are equally difficult to restore and do not provide much help. Felix Jacoby (FGrHist IIIb comm. 223; 1949, 59. 281-82 n. 51) thought that this kind of work started with a historical introduction which gave the stories about the foundation of the games. Perhaps it also provided the further history of the games as more and more contests were added. The main part, the list of the Olympic victors, consisted, according to Jacoby, only of the blank names of victors in the diverse competitions.

Hippias's *Olympionikon anagraphé* was probably written as a literary work. It seems therefore possible that its character was more literary than what we would find in a mere listing of plain names. Plato's Socrates, however, teases Hippias about his learning in historical affairs. Socrates remarks that Hippias must be lucky not being asked by the Lacedaemonians to recite the Athenian archons since Solon. Thus provoked, Hippias boasts that he would memorize 50 names having heard them once (Hippias Maj. 285d–e). This might be an indication that he perhaps was famous for his long list of names. On the other hand, it does not necessarily indicate that he was capable of actually generating long lists of names on his own to mark his putative erudition. Especially if he constructed, and did not deliberately invent, the names of Olympic victors from material such as oral tradition, legendary myths and dedicatory inscriptions, he might have preferred to give the whole story and not only a list of names. We might therefore imagine his work to have originally had a far more narrative character, even though a long history of excerpting has left us with no more than the names.

Not having a single fragment of Hippias's list, it is in fact only Eusebius in the 4th century CE who provides us with the most comprehensive ancient list of Olympic victors. It is found in the first book of his Chronicle, where he presents the collected chronographical material he then used to build his canons, the famous synchronistic tables. This list ends with the 249th Olympiad or the year 217 CE. This is one of the arguments for regarding the lost *chronographiai* of Sextus Julius Africanus, the first Christian chronography from the 3rd century CE, as Eusebius's source for the Olympic victors. The supposition that Eusebius found this list in Africanus's *chronographiai* has been challenged by Mosshammer. Africanus did not use the calculation by Olympiads himself and it is a little surprising that Eusebius, who heavily criticized Africanus, should have trusted his chronographical knowledge (Mosshammer 1979:138–66). If Mosshammer's arguments against Africanus' authorship of the list of Olympic victors in Eusebius are valid, Rutgers's 1862 edition of Africanus's *Olympiadon anagraphé* might well turn out to be a philologist's fiction.

Besides Eusebius's list, parts of the Olympic victor list are preserved in a papyrus from the 3rd century CE (POxy II 222 = FGrHist 415), in fragments of Phlegon of Tralles (FGrHist 257), a *libertus* of Hadrian, and a papyrus from c. 30 BCE (POxy I 12 = FGrHist 255). The rest are literary testimonies about works with titles like *Olympionikon anagraphé*, *Olympionikai*, or *Olympiades* even by famous scholars like Aristotle, Timaeus, and Eratosthenes, of which little or nothing has survived.

Due to the poor, fragmentary state of most Greek historiography outside of Herodotus, Thucydides, Xenophon, and Polybius, it is not easy to determine when the chronographical use of Olympic victors began. Polybius wrote that around 300 BCE, Timaeus established synchronisms between the ephors and kings of Sparta, the archons at Athens, the priestesses at Argos, and the Olympic victors (FGrHist 566 T10 ap. Pol. 12.11). There are fragments of Timaeus showing that he dated events in years before the first Olympic games (such as the synchronized foundations of Rome and Carthage 38 years before the first Olympiad: Dion. Hal. Ant. Rom. 1.74.1 = Timaeus FGrHist 566 F60).

This means, of course, that he would have had an idea when to start counting Olympic victors and that he made attempts to synchronize the first Olympic games with other events. Perhaps he started counting Olympiads by numbers, too. The use of ordinal numbers for Olympiads is, however, attested for the first time in an inscription from the first half of the 3rd century BCE, the so-called Olympiad chronicle from Athens (IG II/III2 2326) (Ebert 1982).

Many modern scholars assume that it was Hippias of Elis who dated the foundation of the Olympic games to a year which we translate as 776 BCE. The discussion about the authenticity of the Olympic victor list is thus essentially connected with the discussion about the foundation date. One line of argument derives from the idea that Hippias found a documentary list starting around 580 BCE (Ol. 50) when some consider that Elis finally took over the sanctuary at Olympia (cf. Möller 2003), and that he therefore had to reconstruct the victors for the earlier games. How did he know where to start?

Mahaffy (1881) thought that Hippias determined the foundation date by Iphitus, the mythical founder of the games, and that the earlier parts of the list, i.e. before the 50th Olympiad, were constructed accordingly. Cavaignac (1913–20:336-9) believed that Hippias had found 40–50 names for the time prior to 580 BCE when the documentary list started. He assumed that till 612 BCE the games were hold annually and calculated that the Olympic games started around 650 BCE. His clearly arbitrary arguments found immediate response (Wade-Gery 1925:762-64). Wilamowitz (1922:481-90) equally doubted the penteteric character of the games right from the beginning and distinguished between the list which he considered authentic and the chronology based on this list. He could therefore claim that the date of 776 BCE was much too high (but see also Jacoby, FGrHist IIIb comm. 152 n. 47 for criticism). These arguments were followed up by Lenschau (1936, 1938:224-27) who took the year 580 BCE as the beginning of penteteric games and assumed that Hippias had found 49 names of victors in the stadium race which prompted him to calculate $(49 \times 4) + 580 = 776 =$ Ol. 1.

That Hippias calculated with these numbers is quite out of the question. How could he have known to add 49x4 to 580 years before the birth of Christ or the beginning of the common era and that the first Olympic games took place accordingly 776 years before the common era started? If Hippias calculated the first Olympic games at all, he could only either synchronize them with another event or estimate an interval between him or another dated event in the past and the first victor. Brouwers (1952) supposed that the Olympic games of 476 were the starting point for the estimation of an interval of 300 years till the first games. This interval, he held, was calculated by means of a Spartan genealogy which had nine generations between Lycurgus who, as was generally believed, helped Iphitus to establish the games and Archidamos who became king in 476 BCE. Both were synchronized by Aristotle's claim to have seen the discus of Iphitus at Olympia (Plut. *Lyc.* 1.2; cf. Paus. 5.20.1). Lycurgus was made soon responsible for co-founding the games (Hieronymus of Rhodes F33 Wehrli ap. Athen. 14.635F).

This argument has some flaws, as normally the Spartan king list was calculated in generations of 40 years, thus not adding up nine generations to 300 years, and there is no evidence for a genealogy having these nine generations before Apollodorus synchronized Lycurgus with the Spartan king Alkamenes (FGrHist 244 F7a–c). The supposed intrinsic connection between Hippias's construction and the date of the first Olympic games is further exploited by Peiser (1990), who believes that the date of 776 BCE is the crime of Hippias, although he acknowledges the impact of later chronography in lengthening the Olympic chronology.

If we remember that there is not a single fragment of Hippias's *Olympionikon anagraphé* left to us, it is rather perplexing that so many arguments about the date of the first Olympic games start from the assumption that Hippias could be made responsible for dating the first games. He probably started his list with Koroibos, the famous first victor of the stadium race who enjoyed hero worship and whose grave was known at the Elian border (Paus. 8.26.3f.), but whether Hippias actually tried to synchronize him with another famous figure is open to discussion. He should have had at least some ideas about a relative chronology of the first games, such as after the return of the Heraclids and long before the synoikism of Elis.

Very likely it was Eratosthenes of Cyrene in the second half of the 3rd century BCE who fixed the beginning of the Olympic games so as to allow us to translate it to the 776th year before Christ's birth or the common era (Bickerman 1980:75-6). Timaeus's Olympiad dating, however, remains too fragmentary to enable us to get a clear idea about his temporal grid, and to allow us to know where exactly he placed the first Olympics. We hear that Timaeus put the Trojan War 417 years before the first Olympiad, whereas Eratosthenes calculated 407 years (Censorinus, De die natali 21.2; Timaeus FGrHist F125; Eratosthenes FGrHist F1c) which makes it likely that they had different estimates either for the fall of Troy or the first Olympiad. We are in fact as ignorant as Dionysius of Halicarnassus about Timaeus's *kanones* (Dion. Hal. Ant. Rom. 1.74.1; cf. Jacoby, FGrHist 566 comm. 538 with n. 97, on Timaeus's and Eratosthenes's dating by Olympiads), whereas Eratosthenes's *kanones* proved remarkably influential. Eratosthenes's fragment 1a, however, provides us with a periodization of Greek history from the fall of Troy down to Alexander's death in 323 BCE.

Eratosthenes [FGrHist 241:F1a] defines the ages as follows:

From the fall of Troy until the return of the Heraclids . . . . 80 years
From these until the settlement of Ionia . . . . 60 years
The time thereafter until Lycurgus' guardianship . . . . 159 years
Until the year preceding the first Olympiad . . . . 108 years
From this Olympiad until the invasion of Xerxes . . . . 297 years
From this until the beginning of the Peloponnesian war . . . . . . 48 years
And until the end of the war and the defeat of the Athenians . . 27 years
And until the battle of Leuktra . . . . 34 years
After this until Philip's death . . . . 35 years
Thereafter until the passing away of Alexander . . . . 12 years

Eratosthenes gives the intervals in years between each event which enable us to calculate from otherwise established absolute dates such as the death of Alexander that Eratosthenes fixed the first Olympic games to a year equivalent to our 776/75 BCE.

How did he calculate this date? To answer this question, it is necessary to take a look at the foundation myth of the Olympic games. Ancient Greeks hold that it was Iphitus who founded the games at Olympia. Unfortunately, this Iphitus did not belong to a proper genealogy, and was thus difficult to date. Only when Aristotle saw the so-called discus of Iphitus at Olympia which bore a text about the institution of the sacred truce and was inscribed with Lycurgus's name, it became possible to synchronize Iphitus with Lycurgus (Plut. Lyc. 1.3). Quite apart from the fact that the Spartan lawgiver Lycurgus changed his position in Greek chronology as he was connected with different kings of the Spartan king list, the synchronism seems to have caused some difficulties with already established dates. Eratosthenes and Apollodorus both maintained that Lycurgus lived a long time before the first Olympiad. Thus, the synchronization of Lycurgus with the foundation of the Olympic games and the statement that he lived long before this event caused a huge gap. Timaeus's solution to this was to assume the existence of two men under the name Lycurgus. This idea is still followed when scholars argue that it was not the Spartan lawgiver, but a homonymous hero who instituted the Olympic truce together with Iphitus (Wilamowitz 1884:284; Jacoby, FGrHist 257 comm. 839).

If one wanted to keep the synchronism and at the same time leave Lycurgus where he was placed by the Spartan king list, one had to cover this gap. A solution was found by inserting the so-called uncounted Olympiads. In Eusebius, we hear of 27 uncounted Olympiads that were not written down in the official lists before the Eleans, the owners of the sanctuary at Olympia and organizers of the festival, started to record each winner of each contest (Eusebius Chron. I 90 Karst). The invention of several uncounted Olympiads helped to keep the synchronism between Lycurgus and Iphitus straight. (The alternative 13 uncounted Olympiads are ascribed to Callimachus who might have had a smaller gap to cover). Weniger (1920/21:44) suggests that he counted eight years for one Olympiad. It seems that Iphitus's foundation of the games was divided from their first victor which enabled the chronographers to keep Iphitus synchronized with Lycurgus. The actual list could then start with the first known and recorded champion. That Iphitus must have reached an age close to Methuselah apparently did not matter.

Back to Eratosthenes, one may see that he put Lycurgus at a distance of 108 years until the year preceding the first Olympiad; 108 divided by 4 makes 27. This should be the same distance of 27 uncounted Olympiads as in Eusebius's much later note. The synchronism between Lycurgus, the Spartan lawgiver, and Iphitus, the founding father of the Olympic games, which became possible after Aristotle had discovered the discus of Iphitus at Olympia, not only enabled Eratosthenes to connect the Spartan king list with the Olympiad era, but also allowed him to assign Lycurgus an authoritative date which reconciled diverging traditions of the Spartan king list and the new Olympiad era (Mosshammer 1979:174–80; cf. den Boer 1954:4–29 for alternative calculations).

It is not especially productive merely to question the date 776 BCE by simply declaring Hippias a liar and inventor of the list of Olympic victors. As we have seen, Hippias himself seems likely not to have had much invested in fixing a foundation date for the games. Rather, it was the later chronographers who seem to have used Hippias' Olympionikon anagraphé in their efforts to turn the first games into the beginning of an era which would give them a fixed position in the temporal coordinate system of Greek chronography.

References

Asheri, David. "The Art of Synchronization in Greek Historiography: the Case of Timaeus of Tauromenium." *Scripta Classica Israelica* 11 (1991/92):52–89.

Beloch, Karl Julius. "Die Siegerliste von Olympia." *Hermes* 64 (1929):192–98.

Bengtson, Hermann. *Die Olympischen Spiele in der Antike* 2nd ed. Zurich: Artemis, 1972.

Bickerman, Elias J. *Chronology of the Ancient World* 2nd ed. Ithaca, NY: Cornell University Press, 1980.

Bilik, Ronald. "Literaturbericht über Hippias von Elis 1980–1995." *Anzeiger fuer die Altertumswissenschaften, Humanistische Gesellschaft Innsbruck* 49 (1996):69–78.

———. "Die Zuverlässigkeit der Frühen Olympionikenliste. Die Geschichte eines Forschungsproblems im chronologischen Überblick." *Nikephoros* 13 (2000):47–62.

Brouwers, A. "Lycurge et la date de la fondation des jeux Olympiques." In *Mélanges G. Smets*. Brussels: Université libre de Bruxelles, 1952, 117–24.

Bultrighini, Umberto. *Pausania e le tradizioni democratiche: Argo ed Elide*. Padua: Editoriale Programma: 1990.

Cavaignac, Eugène. *Histoire de l'antiquité*. Paris: Fontemoing, 1913–20.

Daffinà, P. "Senso del tempo e senso della storia: computi cronologici e storicizzazione del tempo." *Rivista degli Studi Orientali* 61 (1987):1–71.

den Boer, Willem. *Laconian Studies*. Amsterdam: North-Holland, 1954.

Ebert, Joachim. "Die 'Olympische Chronik' IG II/2III 2326." In M. Hillgruber, R. Jakobi, and W. Luppe, eds., *J. Ebert: Agonismata. Kleine Philologische Schriften zur Literatur, Geschichte und Kultur der Antike.* Stuttgart: Teubner, 1982, 237–52.

Finley, M. I., and H. W. Pleket. *The Olympic Games: The First Thousand Years.* London: Chatto & Windus, 1976.

Hedrick, Charles W., Jr. "The Prehistory of Greek Chronography." In V. B. Gorman and E. W. Robinson, eds., *Oikistes: Studies in Honor of A. J. Graham.* Leiden: Mnemosyne suppl. 234, 2002, 13–32.

Henige, David. *The Chronology of Oral Tradition: Quest for a Chimera.* Oxford: Oxford University Press, 1974.

Jacoby, Felix. "Über die entwicklung der griechischen Historiographie und den Plan einer Sammlung der griechischen Historikerfragmente." *Klio* 9 (1909):80–123.

———. *Atthis: the Local Chronicles of Ancient Athens.* Oxford: Clarendon, 1949.

Körte, Alfred. "Die Entstehung der Olympionikenliste." *Hermes* 39 (1904):224–43.

Lenschau, Thomas. "Forschungen zur Griechischen Geschichte im VII. und VI. Jahrhundert v. Chr.: IV. Die Siegerliste von Olympia." *Philologus* 91 (1936):396–411.

———. "Griechische Geschichte. Bericht über das Schrifttum der Jahre 1935-1937." *Jahresbericht über die Fortschritte der Altertumswissenschaften* 64 (1938):209–85.

Mahaffy, J. P. "On the Authenticity of the Olympian Register." *Journal of Hellenic Studies* 2 (1881):164–78.

Mallwitz, Alfred. "Cult and Competition Locations at Olympia." In Wendy J. Raschke, ed., *The Archaeology of the Olympics: The Olympics and Other Festivals in Antiquity*. Madison, WI: University of Wisconsin Press, 1988, 79–109.

———. "Ergebnisse und Folgerungen, bearbeitet von K. Herrmann." In A. Mallwitz, ed., *XI. Bericht über die Ausgrabungen in Olympia*. Bearbeitet von Klaus Herrmann, Berlin: Walter de Gruyter, 1999, 181–284.

Mazzarino, Santo. *Il pensiero storico classico* 3 vols. Bari: Editori Laterza, 1966.

Meyer, Eduard. *Forschungen zur Alten Geschichte* 2 vols. Halle: M. Niemeyer, 1892–99.

Miller, Molly. "Archaic Literary Chronography." *Journal of Hellenic Studies* 75 (1955):54–58.

———. "Herodotus as Chronographer." *Klio* 46 (1965):109–28.

———. *The Sicilian Colony Dates*. Albany, NY: SUNY Press, 1970.

———. *The Thalassocracies: Studies in Chronography II*. Albany, NY: SUNY Press, 1971.

Möller, Astrid. "Der Stammbaum der Philaiden. Über Funktionen der Genealogie bei den Griechen." In M. Flashar, H. J. Gehrke, and E. Heinrich, eds., *Retrospektive: Konzepte von Vergangenheit in der griechisch-römischen antike*. Munich: Biering & Brinkmann, 1996, 17–35.

———. "The Beginning of Chronography: Hellanicus' *Hiereiai*." In N. Luraghi, ed., *The Historian's Craft in the Age of Herodotus*. Oxford: Oxford University Press, 2001, 241–62.

———. "Elis, Olympia und das Jahr 580 v. Chr. Zur Frage der Eroberung der Pisatis." In R. Rollinger and Chr. Ulf, eds., *Griechische Archaik: Interne Entwicklungen – Externe Impulse*. Berlin: Akademie Verlag, 2003, 245–66.

Mosshammer, Alden A. *The Chronicle of Eusebius and Greek Chronographic Tradition*. Lewisburg, PA: Bucknell University Press, 1979.

Pearson, Lionel. *The Local Historians of Attica*. Philological Monographs 11. Philadelphia, PA: American Philological Association, 1942.

Peiser, Benny J. "The Crime of Hippias of Elis: Zur Kontroverse um die Olympionikenliste." *Stadion* 16 (1990):37–65.

Prakken, D. W. *Studies in Greek Genealogical Chronology*. Lancaster, PA: Lancaster Press, 1943.

Rutgers, John. *Sextus Julius Africanus*. [Orig. Leiden: 1862] Chicago: Ares, 1980.

Sinn, Ulrich. *Olympia: Kult, Sport und Fest in der Antike*. Munich: Beck, 1996.

Thomas, Rosalind. *Oral Tradition and Written Record in Classical Athens*. Cambridge: Cambridge University Press, 1989.

Van Compernolle, René. *Étude de chronologie et d'historiographie siciliotes. Recherches sur le système chronologique des sources de Thucydide concernant la fondation des colonies siciliotes*. Brussels: Palais des Académies, 1959.

WadeGery, H. T. "The Growth of the Dorian States." In *Cambridge Ancient History* 3 (1925):527–70, 762–64.

Weniger, Ludwig. "Olympische Studien: Wann wurde die erste Olympiade gefeiert?" *Archiv für Religionswissenschaft* 20 (1920/21):41–78.

Wilamowitz, Ulrich von. *Homerische Untersuchungen*. Philologische Untersuchungen 7. Berlin: Weidmann, 1884.

———. *Pindaros*. Berlin: Weidmann, 1922.

… 9 …

PAGAN AND CHRISTIAN NOTIONS OF THE WEEK IN THE 4TH CENTURY CE WESTERN ROMAN EMPIRE

Michele Renee Salzman

Almost anywhere we travel in the world today, we can count on living by the seven-day week. This was not always so. In the only extant 4th century Roman calendar to survive, the Codex Calendar of 354, there were no fewer than three "weekly cycles," one of eight-days, to record the traditional Roman market week, one of seven-days to record the planetary week, and one of 10 days to record the lunar cycle. The conjunction of no fewer than three different weekly cycles in a calendar filled with pagan holidays and intended for use by a Christian in the city of Rome in 354 raises some obvious questions, not the least of which is to wonder how prevalent was the notion of the seven-day week in the 4th century.

This question becomes more intriguing since most scholars see the 4th century CE as the time when the seven-day week, culminating with a day off on Sunday, became the accepted way of organizing and minding time. Scholars point to a famous law of March 3, 321 (*Theodosian Code* 2.8.1), in which Constantine made the *dies Solis*—the day of the Sun or Sunday as we call it—a holiday; many scholars see this law as a response to the Christian view of Sunday, and especially the view of the Church of Rome that had been intent on implementing a seven-day weekly cycle anchored on Sunday as a day of worship and/or rest (Bacchiocchi 1977; Zerubavel 1985; Rordorf 1968; Cotton 1933; Beckwith and Stott 1978).

Some scholars have wondered if Constantine, brilliant politician that he was, was not playing both sides of the fence, choosing to recognize a day—*dies Solis*—that was also significant for pagan worshipers, especially those of Sol Invinctus and Mithras, of which there were many more than Christians at the time that Constantine passed his law (Böhmer 1931; Zöckler 1912; Rordorf 1968; Bacchiocchi 1977; Cameron and Hall 1999; de Giovanni 1977). However we interpret Constantine's intentions behind his Sunday law, his actions have led Charles Pietri (1984) and others to argue that it was the 4th century Christians who largely developed and promulgated our modern notion of the seven-day week with its focus on Sunday as a day of rest and worship.

But, given the evidence of the Codex Calendar of 354, with its seven-day week illustrated by pagan astrological signs for a Christian to use—one cannot help but wonder if the notion of the seven-day week anchored on Sunday as promulgated by 4th century Christian leaders and emperors was distinctly different from the notion of the week held by pagans in the Western Roman empire. And further, how did the imperial and Christian emphasis on and view of Sunday contribute to developing the seven-day week in the 4th century Western Roman empire? And finally, given the multiple weekly cycles in the Codex Calendar of 354 did the seven-day week replace other ways of dating and organizing people's time in the 4th century? If not, when did the seven-day week take on these functions in the west?

These three concerns are of more than mere antiquarian interest, for they highlight, among other issues, the ways in which Christians used time to shape their group identity. Indeed, some scholars have argued that Christian leaders focused on Sunday and the seven-day week to establish a unique identity over and against not only Jews, who celebrated the Sabbath, but also pagans (Goldenberg 1979:442-45; Stern 2000:106-107; Zerubavel 1985:22). If, however, the seven-day week and the religious and ritual import of Sunday were already predominant among pagans, Christian leaders do not so much appear to be establishing a separate identity as maintaining continuities with their pagan contemporaries. At issue is the question of the dynamics of group formation and the conversion techniques adopted by the post-Constantinian church.

This chapter argues three main points. First, pagan and Christian notions of the week in the 4th century were very similar, and, in this fluid world, pagans and Christians influenced one another in their use of time as an organizing principle of social life, leaving a legacy that has shaped our contemporary notions of temporality. Second, the recognition of Sunday as a day not only of worship but of rest was a Constantinian innovation which shows Christian influence but had no clear pagan precedents; this helps to explain why this notion of Sunday only gradually shaped 4th century notions of the day for pagans and Christians alike. And third, the notion of the seven-day week with its focus on Sunday cannot be securely documented as replacing other ways of dating or organizing time in the 4th century. Rather, dating by lunar days as well as market days and by Kalends, Nones, and Ides continued throughout this century and well into the next. In other words, it took more than a week, indeed, more than a century, for the effects of Constantine's law and the Christian notion of Sunday as the anchor to the seven-day week to uniformly replace other ways of minding time.

The Seven-day Week: Background

We shall look briefly at the origins of the seven-day week in the Roman Empire in the centuries before Constantine. As Eviatar Zerubavel pointed out in his insightful study, *The Seven-Day Circle* (1985), the seven-day week is not a natural cycle. So, "from an historical standpoint, there are two ways of explaining why the week to which we adhere is seven-days long, neither of which necessarily excludes the other. One explanation relates the length of our week to the seven-days of Creation in traditional Jewish cosmology" (6). The biblical account of Creation explains God's commandment to work for six days and then rest periodically on the seventh day, which for the Jews was the Sabbath. This divine temporal plan requires no further explanation for a believer.

The second way to explain the seven-day cycle relates to the seven planets of ancient astrology: "It is generally believed that the linking of the planets to the seven gods of each day was a Babylonian, or Chaldaean contribution, evolving around 500 BCE in conjunction with astrological needs to cast horoscopes" (14). This linkage may go back to earlier Babylonian beliefs in a universe that was a "sevenfold entity governed by a fusion of seven deities" (7). It is not until the Hellenistic Age that we see evidence for a seven-day astrological week, evolving probably around the 2nd century BCE in Alexandria (Maas 1902:267; Neugebauer 1963:168–69; Boll 1912).

This astrological origin, along with the Egyptian worship of the Sun, may explain why the 2nd century CE Roman historian Dio Cassius (37.18–19) thought that the Egyptians originated the seven-day planetary week that spread in the Roman Empire in the 1st century BCE. The earliest Roman reference to the gods of the week comes from the 1st century BCE poet Tibullus, who claims to have used as a pretext for lingering with his lover, the "sacred day of Saturn" (1.3.18).

From this point on, the names of the planetary days of the week can be found in a variety of Roman writers. Often, as in the *Satires* of Juvenal, these references are tied to astrological predictions, or to the Sabbath observance of the Jews (*Sat.* 7.160; 14.96 ff.; see Meinhold 1909; Boll 1912:2573–74). We hear of teachers of rhetoric giving their lessons on a seven-day weekly basis, be it Fridays in Juvenal's Rome (*Sat.* 7.160) or Saturdays in Suetonius's Rhodes (*Tiberius* 32.4). By the 2nd century, Dio Cassius can claim that the seven-day planetary week is becoming quite habitual to all the rest of mankind and to the Romans themselves: "The custom of referring the days to the seven stars called planets was instituted by the Egyptians. . . But since it is now quite the fashion with mankind generally and even with the Romans themselves, and is to them already in a way an ancestral tradition, I wish to write briefly of it" (37.18.1–2).

Such familiarity was based on more than mere speech habits; by the 1st century CE, we see clear evidence that the Romans were using the seven-day planetary week to keep track of their dates; three of 43 calendars extant from the 1st century CE published by Atillio Degrassi (1963:326) included the letters A–G for the days of the seven-day planetary week alongside the letters A–H for the eight-day market week.

A utilitarian function is indicated too, in the more abbreviated calendars that have come down to us, known as *parapegmata*. An example of one, from a wall adjacent to the Baths of Trajan in Rome, was preserved even after that building became a small Christian sanctuary to Saint Felicity; in it the days of the week are indicated by the planets, whose seven busts are depicted at the top above a zodiac circle. The zodiac circle was used to show the 12 months of the year. To the left and right are the days of the lunar month (see Figure 9.1). A bone peg found with this parapegma allowed the user to indicate the weekly and monthly cycle. In several of these abbreviated calendars, the seven-day week is accompanied by the eight-day market cycle recorded by the name of the town (Degrassi 1963:299–307; Salzman 1990:8–10).

That people referred to events in their own lives using the planetary names is shown by inscriptions from private monuments. In Hermann Dessau's 1892–1916 collection *Inscriptiones Latinae Selectae* (hereafter cited as *ILS*) of almost 10,000 Latin inscriptions, some nine monuments date events using the planetary named days. Some of these are funerary monuments giving the date of death in this manner, perhaps because the day of death was thought to have been determined by the movement of the planets. Yet, even in these, the date of death is also recorded according to the conventional system of Kalends, Nones, and Ides. So, for example, the pagan from Rome, Blastio, notes his birthday on the Kalends of September, on the sixth hour of the Day of the Moon, or Monday, and his death date, three days before the ides of June, in the first hour of the day of Saturn, our Saturday (Dessau *ILS*:8528).

The association of the days of the week with astrological and cosmic ties is also noteworthy within the context of the cult of Mithras; a Mithras worshiper in 202 claimed that he was "born at dawn in the consulship of the two Augusti, Severus and Antoninus, twelve days before the Kalends of December [i.e., 20 November, 202], on the day of Saturn, on the eighteenth day of the moon," as Vermaseren notes in his *Corpus Inscriptionum et Monumentorum Religionis Mithrae* (1956:no. 498; hereafter cited as *CIMRM*; see also Vermaseren and van Essen 1965). Some scholars have interpreted this to refer to his rebirth through some sort of Mithraic initiation (Clauss 2000:104-105; Guarducci 1979). But what is noteworthy is the use of three dating conventions, Kalends, Nones, and Ides, the planetary week, and the lunar cycle, as well as the standard dating by consular year.

The widespread interest in astrology certainly contributed to the growing familiarity with the seven-day planetary week, judged by the frequency with which we find references to these in texts and calendars from the Roman Empire in the 2nd and 3rd centuries. But some scholars, like Paul Marie Duval (1953), have argued that it was also the popular pagan cults of Mithras and Sol that, in this period, help explain the growing importance of the seven-day planetary week. Robert Turcan has maintained that the week had liturgical import for Mithraists, based in part on the symbolic ladder of the planets which, according to Celsus (Origen, *Contra Celsum* 6.22) was shown to initiates and represented a week going backward, starting from the day of Saturn (Saturday) and ending with the day of Sol (Sunday) (Turcan 1993:100). A Mithraic relief from Bologna also

Figure 9.1 Parapegma Urbanum Thermarum Triaiani (early 2nd century CE). Image from A. Degrassi, Inscriptiones Italiae. Volumen XIII Fasti et Elogia Fasciculus II, Libreria dello Stato, Rome, 1963, 309

shows the gods of the week, but beginning with Sol (from right to left) (Vermaseren *CIMRM*:693). Turcan explains the placement of Sol in the Bologna relief as being tied to notions of Mithras as the god of Time and to Pythagorean influences on the developing Mithraic cult; according to Turcan (but with no supporting evidence), the Pythagoreans consecrated the seventh day to Apollo, that is Sol, and this, in conjunction with the close association of Sol Invictus with Mithras explains the sequence of the planets beginning with Sol, not Saturn, in the Bologna relief. Yet another reason for this placement may be the practices of astrologers; the 2nd century astrologer Vettius Valens, in his *Anthologiarum* 1.10 (Kroll 1908: 26), reckoned birth dates using a seven-day week beginning with Sol, not Saturn.

The evidence that can be adduced for the Mithraists' use of the seven-day planetary week is largely iconographic; we simply do not know how much it shaped their liturgy in the centuries before Constantine. So, while it seems logical that Mithraists should incorporate the seven-day week given its planetary base and the iconographic remains from Mithraea, there is no firm evidence, as far as we can know, that they actually did so. This is also true for the cult of Sol Invictus, which was, as noted above, so closely linked with that of Mithras in the popular mind that people made vows to Sol Invictus Mithras (Vermaseren *CIMRM*:360–62; see Halsberghe 1972). The most we can say is that some pagans, as well as some Christians in the second and third centuries, used the seven-day weekly cycle to date moments in their private lives, but they did so in conjunction with other dating conventions.

Pagan and Christian Notions of the Seven-day Week in the 4th Century

The Roman habit of using multiple dating conventions continued into the 4th century, despite the noticeably heightened level of rhetoric used by Christian preachers against the astrological and pagan associations of the seven-day planetary week. Indeed, Christian leaders vehemently attacked the clearly widespread notion that the planetary days influenced people's lives. The manual by the African mathematician Hilarius, *De Solstitiis*, dated to the fourth or fifth century, may be seen as representative of the types of arguments made at the time (Dekkers and Gaar 1961:n. 2277). The Christians, Hilarius claimed, were freed from planetary influences, for the stars are not independent forces of nature, but the signs placed by the creator for the computation of time. Christ, the Son of Justice, was born in December (*De Solstitiis PLS* 1.567). The bishop Ambrose, another Christian preacher interested in this topic, used this same reasoning to explain how different and superior are Christian calculations of time from pagan ones (Saint Ambrose, *Letters* 23.4; *PL* 16.1027; *Hexameron* 4.6.25). And the late 4th century writer Ambrosiaster (*Quaestiones* 84) saw Christian time reckoning as superior because, even though both pagans and Christians use lunar days, Christians know that they use lunar days because they were given by God to establish the signs of the times, not because they determine the nature of the day as auspicious or not. Since Ambrosiaster notes the use of lunar days as acceptable, his text indicates too that the habit of using the lunar cycle alongside the seven-day cycle persisted well into the late 4th and early 5th centuries.

The vehemence of the Christian stand against the astrological associations of the seven-day week is even more understandable when we consider that in the fourth century, some Manicheans, like the African Faustus, accused the Christians of adoring the sun and the moon (Augustus *Contra Faustum* 15.2, 18.5; see also Pietri 1984). Indeed, to counter this claim, some Christian leaders recommended avoiding the astrological nomenclature of the week completely; Philaster of Brescia in his *Liber Adversus Omnes Haereses* accused those who think of the days of the week with their planetary names (e.g. *dies Saturni*, *dies Solis*) as heretics (113; *CC* 279).

While some Christian preachers accepted the traditional nomenclature for the seven-day week, others advocated using more religiously sensitive language. In particular, they advocated calling Sunday *dies Dominica*, the Lord's day, and then numbering each successive day accordingly (i.e., the first day *feria prima*, the second day *feria secunda*, etc.). In his *Commentary on the Psalms*, Augustine urged that Christians be corrected when they referred to a day as belonging to a deity, like that "of Mercury," and should instead call it the fourth day, since Christians "have their own language for such things" (*Enarrationes in Psalmos* 93.3; *CCSL* 39, p.1302). And in the middle of the 5th century, the Christian Polemius Silvius removed the planetary letters as well as names of the days of the week from his calendar following along a similar line of reasoning (Degrassi 1963:263–77). Indeed, the Gallic bishop, Caesarius of Arles, was even more vociferous in condemning the planetary days of the week; he cajoled his followers to refrain from using such "demonic" terms, and to instruct their families to do the same (*Sermo* 193.4; *CCSL* 104: 756-86)).

Yet even the most self-conscious of Christian preachers at times found themselves slipping back into using the planetary names for the days of the week; Jerome justified this habit by arguing, among other things, that Christians can accept the pagan name *dies Solis*, since that was the day on which the light of the world appeared (*In die dominica Paschae CC* 78: 56). From such remarks it is clear that for both pagans and Christians in the 4th century, the seven-day week remained closely tied to its astrological roots, and the notion that the planets influenced people on a daily basis remained widespread.

Sunday: Imperial and Christian Influences

But if pagans and Christians shared this astrological view of the seven-day week, can the same be said for 4th century notions about how to celebrate Sunday? To answer this, we need to step back in time once more to look at evidence for Sunday among pagans and Christians in the centuries before Constantine.

Here we find a significant difference between pagans and Christians, for despite the recurrent assumption in modern scholarship about the importance of the *dies Solis* in paganism, there is no good evidence to indicate that pagans celebrated the *dies Solis* as a religious holiday. There are, however, clear indications that the Christians prior to Constantine did view Sunday as a day for ritual and prayer.

Sunday before Constantine

We have already considered some of the iconographic evidence that suggests that Sol within the context of the planetary week was especially important to Mithraists as well as to followers of Sol Invictus in the centuries before Constantine. Some evidence exists that Mithraists did celebrate important movements of the sun in the sky at certain points throughout the year; that was what a group of Mithras worshipers in Virunum in Noricum in the late second century did at the summer solstice (Beck 1998). This is not surprising, perhaps, since the winter solstice was popularly celebrated across the Eastern and Western Empire; in Rome, on December 25th, the Anniversary of the Sun, *Natalis Solis*, was celebrated with numerous circus games, probably ever since the time of Aurelian in the late 3rd century (Salzman 1990:149–53).

Some scholars, most notably Turcan (1993:100) and Chastagnol (1978), have posited the idea that some Mithras worshipers, and perhaps some Sol Invictus worshipers, influenced by Pythagorean ideals, celebrated the *dies Solis* in the 3rd century. But an examination of the Mithraic inscriptions in *CIMRM*, combined with an examination of the Sol Invictus inscriptions in Halsberghe's collection as well as those in Dessau's collection, *Inscriptiones Latinae Selectae*, provides no secure evidence to support the notion that the day of the Sun was ritually commemorated by Mithraic worshipers or Pythagoreanists on a weekly basis (Vermaseren 1956; Halsberge 1972).

The only evidence for pagans commemorating a day of the week in honor of Sol comes from the Christian apologist, Tertullian. In a passage from his *Ad Nationes*, Tertullian defends Christians against the charge of Sun-worshiping by claiming that some pagans in Carthage honored Sol by abstaining or delaying bathing, by resting and by feasting. The passage is worth quoting:

> 13. 3. Vos certe estis, qui etiam in laterculum septem dierum solem recepistis, et [. . .] ex diebus ipsorum praelegistis, quo die lavacrum subtrahatis aut in vesperam differatis, aut otium et prandium curetis. 4. Quod quidem facitis exorbitantes et ipsi a vestris ad alienas religiones: Iudaei enim festi sabbata et cena pura et Iudaici ritus lucernarum et ieiunia cum azymis et orationes litorales, quae utique aliena sunt a diis vestris. 5. Quare, ut ab excessu revertar, qui solem et diem eius nobis exprobratis, agnoscite vicinitatem; non longe a Saturno et sabbatis vestris sumus!
>
> [13.3. You [pagans] are clearly the ones who have accepted the sun as one of the seven-days of the week and [. . .] have selected this one day over other days as the day on which you do not take a bath or you postpone it until the evening, or you take care to give yourself some rest and a meal. 4. By resorting to these customs, you are deviating from your own rites to those of others; indeed the Jewish feasts are the Sabbath and the "purificatory dinner" and the ceremonies of the lamps and fasting with unleavened bread and littoral prayers, which are very alien from your gods. 5. You who reproach us with the sun and the day, recognize your proximity: we are not far from your Saturn and your Sabbaths!] (1.13.1–5)*

---

* I followed the text of Andre Schneider, *Le Premier Livre Ad Nationes de Tertullien, Introduction, Texte, Traduction et Commentaire*. Rome: Institut Suisse, 1968. Schneider accepts a *crux* before *ex diebus* and reads: "et [. . .] ex diebus ipsorum praelegistis" as evidence for Sunday celebrations.

The crucial sentence in section 13.3 indicating that pagans honored Sol on Sunday has been called into question on several accounts. First, there are textual problems in the manuscripts in the line before Tertullian's claim that pagans honor Sol on Sunday. Indeed, all scholars accept a crux in the manuscript, but there are diverging opinions as to how to reconstruct the text. Some scholars (Bacchioni 1977:248–51) read it as evidence for pagan worship on Sundays, while others would emend the passage to read it as evidence that pagans honor "the day preceding the day of the sun," that is Saturday, not Sunday (Rordorf 1968:32–38; Chastagnol 1978). Indeed, this second reading would fit more comfortably with the remainder of the passage, for Tertullian goes on to assert that pagans are indulging in Jewish practices on the Sabbath, and that Christians are close to these Sabbath practices. Moreover, we have ample testimony that some pagans did mark the Sabbath, the day of Saturn; these pagans were motivated either by reverence for the influence of the planet Saturn as the first day of the astrological week, or in imitation of the Jews; in Tertullian's *Apologeticus* Chapter 16, where Tertullian is once again defending Christians against the charge of being Sun worshipers, Tertullian notes that Christians who devote Sunday to rejoicing, "have some resemblance to those of you who devote the day of Saturn to ease and luxury" (See also Flavius Josephus *Contra Apion* 2.39.282). And finally, in a passage that actually contradicts his previous testimony in *Ad Nationes* 13.3, Tertullian in *De Idolatria* 14.7 claims that pagans do not have weekly holidays, only annual ones.

Certainty about the meaning of Tertullian's evidence in *Ad Nationes* 13.3 thus seems impossible, but even if we accept a reading of that text as evidence for pagan practices on Sunday, the most we can say is that some pagans in Carthage, presumably following solar or Christian practice, marked Sunday as special with informal observances (such as abstention from bathing, feasting, or resting). It is clear that such observances were not at all uniform; even in Carthage in the 3rd century, some pagans recognized the day of Saturn, our

Saturday, as a special day of the week, either because it was the first day of the astrological week and/or in imitation of Jewish practice. Thus Saturn was depicted first in the Codex Calendar of 354 (Salzman 1990:30–31). Moreover, if the pagan observances noted by Tertullian on Sunday extended beyond Carthage, there has been no trace of them identified in other texts.

In contrast, Sunday was the object of pastoral attention among Christians, as early, some have argued, as the end of the 1st century, when Ignatius, in Rome, wrote letters to various Churches, in which he spoke of his Jewish converts as "no longer observing Sabbaths, but living in accordance with the Lord's day" (*Epistle to the Magnesians*; see also *Epistle to Barnabas* and *Teachings of the Twelve Apostles*). Clearer evidence of such practice is found in Justin who, in the mid-2nd century, writes in his *Apology* to the emperor: "The day of the Sun, we assemble, because it is the first day, on which God . . . created the world and because on this day Jesus Christ, our Savior, came back from the dead" (1.67.6). The association with Christ's resurrection on Easter Sunday was echoed in later writers. Moreover, according to Willy Rordorf (1968:238–73), who argued from the textual evidence provided by Justin and Pliny, the 2nd century most likely also saw a change from a Sunday evening worship meeting to an early Sunday morning one, before daybreak.

The evidence from the 3rd century also indicates that Sunday had not become the uniform day for prayer across the empire's Christian communities. Although Tertullian strongly advocates Sunday as the only day for prayer among Christians in third century North Africa, he also shows that some Christians there, as still in many parts in the East, still followed the Jewish practice of special prayers on Sabbath mornings as well as on Sunday mornings (*De Oratione* 23.1). Indeed, Tertullian vehemently decries this practice and the willingness of Christians to mark the Sabbath by fasting (*De Jejuniis* 14ff.). His hostility toward Sabbath observances is echoed in Rome by Hippolytus who, in the early third century, also preached against this practice (*Comm. In Dan.* 4.20). The intent of both

Tertullian and Hippolytus seems clear: both wish to distinguish Christian religious observances from the Jewish traditions of the Sabbath and would focus on Sunday alone, not Saturday, as the day for prayer. Although this had not yet happened in the 3rd century, it was the focus of considerable Christian energy. Interestingly, none of the third century sources I have seen, nor those surveyed by Rordorf in his magisterial study of Sunday in the early Church, indicate that Christians advocated making Sunday into a day of rest among Christians; rather, their focus was on the religious rituals and prayer appropriate to Sunday as the "Lord's day" (Rordorf 1968:161; 1972). Hence work on the remainder of Sunday was not prohibited.

Sunday: Constantine and After

The pre-Constantinian emphasis on the part of certain Christian bishops on Sunday as a day for worship helps to explain why Constantine's law of March 3, 321, to Helpidius, *vicarius* of Rome, made the day of the Sun a legal holiday, "celebrated on account of its own veneration" (*Theodosian Code* 2.8.1). In accord with Roman practice, Constantine stipulated that legal transactions not be conducted on this day. So, as early as 325, we see a judge deferring a law case in Egypt because the proceedings would fall on Sunday (Llewelyn and Nobbs 2002). However, according to the *Theodosian Code*, acts of manumission and the emancipation of slaves, which could now take place in church, were allowed on Sundays (2.8.1). In the version of this law that survives in the *Justinianic Code*, Constantine goes even further than traditional Roman holiday practice would require, indicating that not only judges, but even the urban plebs and artisans of all types should rest on the venerable day of the Sun; only agricultural workers are singled out for exception, being advised to take advantage of good weather (*Codex Justinianus* 3.12.2). And market days, with their festival atmosphere, when schools were normally closed, could be held on Sundays as well

(*Corpus Inscriptionum Latinarum* 3.4121; and for schools, see Andreau 2000). Yet, although Constantine made Sunday a legal holiday, none of his extant legislation stipulates the pre-Constantinian Christian idea that Sunday be a time to worship. Moreover, Constantine referred to this holiday as *dies Solis*—literally the day of the Sun—not by the already available Christian alternative—*dies Dominica*. Hence, he used language that pagans were familiar with from astrology and from the seven-day planetary week recorded in Roman calendars.

The language in Constantine's law has perplexed some scholars and fueled the desire to assess not only the impact of the law but its intent. Constantine's biographer, Eusebius of Caesarea, in his *Life of Constantine*, sees only Christianizing fervor on the part of the emperor: "He decreed that the truly sovereign and really first day, the day of the Lord and Savior, should be considered a regular day of prayer" (4.18.1). But Eusebius's testimony suggests that Constantine's law was more ambiguous than this statement would allow, for Eusebius continues in this passage to claim that a second decree of Constantine had ordered all Christian soldiers to "revere the Day of Salvation, which also bears the name of Light Day or Sun Day" by attending Church and ordered all those who were not Christian to go "out of the city" to pray to a nameless god of victories (4.18.1). Eusebius leaves the impression that this decree covered the whole army, but, as the most recent commentators to this *Life* have observed, it was probably only Constantine's garrison at Constantinople who were led "out of the city" to pray (Cameron and Hall 1999:318). Moreover, Eusebius tells us that the emperor urged these soldiers to "lift up their hands to heaven," and "extend their mental vision yet higher [i.e., to the Sun] to the heavenly King" (*Life* 4.19).

Despite Eusebius's attempt to present Constantine's actions as consonant with Christian beliefs, the lifting of the hands to the heavens and the exhortation to a nameless god of victories have suggested to many that Constantine was aiming to appeal to pagan worshipers of Sol Invictus; indeed, if Eusebius's text can be believed, the men in the army at Constantinople saw it this way. In this act,

Constantine may have been following in the footsteps of his rival, Licinius, who had used such monotheistic prayers to encourage his army in fighting against Maximin Daia (Bacchiocchi 1977:247–69; Cameron and Hall 1999: 318).

Although there is no clear evidence that the *dies Solis* was recognized as a pagan holiday before Constantine, pagans would see the institution of such an official celebration as the emperor's prerogative; that is what Aurelian had presumably done for Sol Invictus in the late third century in instituting the *Natalis Solis* (see Halsberghe 1972:131–55). The language of the law—"the day of the sun deserves veneration"—would have appealed to Sol and Mithras worshipers; indeed, there is no evidence to suggest that pagans were offended at what appears a truly innovative holiday established by Constantine. But, in 321, it also seems clear that Constantine was eager to unite the Western Church behind him before going off to fight Licinius in the East. The clergy in Rome and Italy were especially eager to make Sunday—not the Sabbath—the Christian day of worship (Bacchiocchi 1977:207–12). Thus, the 321 law appears as one of a number of laws that shows Constantine's willingness to shape his cult to his immediate political demands.

It is not until some 65 years later that we hear in law an emperor specifying that Sunday is intended as a holiday for Christians; and not until then do we find emperors showing a heightened sensitivity to the pagan associations of the language of the planetary week. In a law of Gratian, Valentinian and Theodosius in 386, we hear that the "day of the Sun [*dies Solis*] which our ancestors rightly called the Lord's Day [*dies Dominica*]," be a public holiday with no court business or legal suits. Moreover, this 386 law is the first extant law to indicate that worship was expected on this day: "That person shall be adjudged not only infamous but also sacrilegious who turns from the inspiration and ritual of holy religion" (*Theodosian Code* 2.18.1). The importance of Sunday for Christians also emerges in a law dated between 368 and 373 which stipulated that "no Christian be sued by a tax collector on Sunday, a day which has long been considered holy, or propitious" (*Theodosian Code* 8.8.1).

Still, the more traditional, pagan notion of Sunday —not as a day of prayer and veneration but as a Roman holiday— persisted throughout 4th century imperial law. Not until 392 were circus games prohibited on the festal days of the Sun, and even then, exceptions were made for the birthdays of the emperors. Imperial games were only prohibited by Theodosius and Honorius in 409 (*Theodosian Code* 2.8.20, 392 CE; 2.8.25, 409 CE). It had taken some 90 years since Constantine first ushered in Sunday as a legal holiday for the pagan idea of how to celebrate a Roman holiday in honor of the Sun to be removed from imperial law.

Sunday: A New Way of Organizing Time?

The gradual implementation of the Christian notion of Sunday as a day of worship—not circus games—leads to my final area for discussion: did the seven-day week, anchored on Sunday, replace other methods used for dating and organizing peoples' lives in the 4th century? We know that people had already used the seven-day week as a dating convention in private inscriptions from the second and thirrd centuries and in some calendars and parapegmata. But people tended to use the seven-day cycle alongside other dating conventions, that is, along with dating by Kalends, Nones, and Ides, by the market cycle usually of eight days, and/or by the lunar cycle of ten days. But, can we see a real change in use and in convention in the 4th century, under the pressure of Constantine's laws and the preaching by Christian leaders about the importance of reconfiguring the days of the seven-day week around the *dies Dominica*? Or, to put it more simply, how much more did the people of the 4th century use the seven-day week to organize activities in their lives?

To try to answer both of these questions, Charles Pietri in an influential article in 1984 looked at a body of 150 Christian funerary inscriptions from Rome (70%) and Italy (30%) that mention the days of the week. He claimed that Christians particularly noted the days of the week, indicating Fridays (32 times) and Sundays (31) most often, followed by Saturdays (21), Thursdays (21), Wednesdays (19), Mondays (17), and last, Tuesdays (9). Christians preferred to use *dies Dominica* (or the Greek equivalent, *hemera kyriake*) to *dies Solis*. This body of inscriptions showed one person out of 30 referring to a day of the week. Moreover, Pietri claimed, this number increased over time. More than half of the inscriptions are from the period 366–440. So, Pietri (1984) concluded, "Everything indicates that this specifically Christian habit introduced itself into the funerary formulae of the 4th century and increased noticeably thereafter" (77). On the basis of this analysis, Pietri argued that it was the Christians who adopted the language of the seven-day week and were hence responsible for making it, along with Sunday as a day of worship, normative practice as early as the middle of the fourth century.

It is surprising that Pietri did no comparative work on pagan inscriptions from Rome and Italy to make his case secure. And, as he himself noted, his corpus of 150 Christian inscriptions was weighted toward the most faithful, being drawn from catacombs and churches. Thus, Pietri's assumptions about the willingness of Christians to adopt the seven-day week were not tested against a comparable group of pagan inscriptions in order to say with any degree of certainty that Christians over and above pagans adopted the seven-day week in their funerary monuments.

There are difficulties in pursuing such a comparison of contemporary pagan inscriptions, not the least of which is the survival of inscriptions from non-Christian contexts in the 4th century and the conversion of the population at large. But given these limitations, some comparative analysis can be undertaken. There are several collections of inscriptions from the most active pagan cults in Rome and Italy in the 4th century. I examined specific collections for four of these cults—Mithras, Isis, Magna Mater, and Sol—as well as the use of dating terminology in the 10,000 inscriptions from H. Dessau's

Inscriptiones Latinae Selectae and in the thousands of inscriptions from the *Corpus Inscriptionum Latinarum*, Volume 6 from Rome. The pagan inscriptions I isolated included: 220 Isis and Sarapis inscriptions from Rome and Italy (Vidman 1969:189–271), 478 Magna Mater inscriptions from Rome and Italy (Vermaseren 1977), the collection of Sol inscriptions from Rome and Italy by Halsberghe which included seven inscriptions specifically dated to the fourth century (Halsberghe 1972:162–75), and 603 Mithraic inscriptions from Italy (Vermaseren *CIMRM*). I also isolated numerous pagan inscriptions in *ILS*, and in the inscriptions from CIL VI indexed in *Corpus Inscriptionum Latinarum* VI part 7. 2 (ed. Jory and Moore 1975); this last collection included over twenty pages of references to *dies* but only four new inscriptions recording the day of the week (i.e., *dies Saturni*, *dies Lunae*, *dies Mercurii*, and *dies Iovis*).

My examination of the epigraphic evidence from the Latin West was not restricted to funerary monuments, as Pietri's had been, but included dedicatory as well as honorific monuments. I found that when pagans did include dates in their inscriptions, by and large they used the traditional dating by Kalends, Nones, and Ides along with consular year. On funerary monuments, the convention was to include the length of life, and if the date of death was included, it was generally so noted by Kalends, Nones, and Ides. Those funerary inscriptions noting the days of the week made up a very small group, no more than forty all told. Hence, my overview of pagan inscriptions would seem to support Pietri's claim that Christians were more open to using the seven-day week in their inscriptions than were their pagan peers in the fourth century.

Why some 4th century Christians noted the days of the week in their funerary inscriptions is worth considering. Unlike pagans, Christians tended to note the date of death and/or date of burial (*depositio*) on their monuments for theological reasons; the day of death and/or day of burial represented the beginning of a new life, an anniversary (*natalis*) by traditional Roman thinking (Ferrua 1920; Grossi Gondi 1920).

But the habit of noting death or burial by the day of the planetary week suggests other influences. Some scholars have explained this practice by emphasizing the on-going influence of astrology on 4th century Christians who would view the planet of their "birth" into a new life as still exercising influence over them after death.(Schürer 1905). Others would explain this epigraphic habit by emphasizing the influence of the Jewish seven-day week (Kajanto 1977). Still others would emphasize the exertions made by Christian bishops who were eager to change the astrological beliefs of their flocks by stressing the seven-day week revolving around the Lord's Day; their efforts would then be seen as key to developing this particular epigraphic habit among 4th century Christians (Pietri 1984).

Even if Christians did use the days of the seven-day week in their funerary monuments more readily than pagans, they—like their pagan peers—continued to use the other conventional ways of dating by Kalends, Nones, and Ides and by consular year. The nomenclature for the seven-day week did not replace traditional dating conventions in these fourth century Christian inscriptions; rather, the days of the week were added to the inscriptions, and only in a relatively small number of cases, as had been the case in the small number of pre-Constantinian pagan examples (Handley 2003).

A more important limitation on Pietri's view of the importance of the Christian epigraphic habit lies in the nature of the evidence. Neither these funerary monuments nor the 4th century imperial laws can tell us what we want to know about how people minded their time, that is how much more than before did fourth century people rely on the seven-day week— rather than the eight day market cycle or the ten day lunar cycle— to organize and schedule their daily lives. Here, we must turn to sparse, anecdotal evidence.

The *Codex Calendar of 354,* with its three weekly cycles of seven, eight, and ten days each, suggests that the seven day week had not yet gained a monopoly over the way people organized their time. Random references to the ongoing use of lunar days and hence ten day lunar cycles is documented for the fourth and fifth centuries. (See the Parapegma from the Baths of Trajan in A. Degrassi 1963:299, 326, and references to lunar days by Ambrosiaster, *Quaestiones* 84). The evidence for market cycles is of interest, for it provides another important way for people to allocate commercial and social time.

Both seven-and eight-day market cycles have a long history in the Roman empire, and there is evidence to suggest that both cycles coexisted into the 4th century. The eight-day market cycle was in use first; its appearance in an official, military context in 3rd century Dura-Europus is one indicator of how wide spread it had become in Roman life (Snyder: 1936). The seven-day market cycle emerged alongside the eight-day one in the first century CE in Campania (Andreau 2000: 88–91). Interestingly, these were not the only two cycles for organizing markets; in North Africa, markets were held on either a 12-or 18-day cycle (Shaw 1981). Elsewhere, they could be held on a twice-monthly basis (de Ligt 1993). These variations in market frequency indicate that market cycles varied by region. The effort to establish a seven-day market in the newly rebuilt town of Aquae Iasae, Pannonia, at the time of Constantine has earlier precedents, and fits easily with this emperor's professed goal of making Sunday and the seven day week the primary means of organizing time in the 4th century (Andreau 2000 for earlier precedents; Shaw 1981:45). However, it is of interest that the establishment of a seven day market cycle is at odds with the Christian and allegedly Constantinian notion that Sunday be a day of worship and rest.

The seven-day cycle was familiar in private and, after Constantine's recognition of Sunday as a holiday, was becoming increasingly important within legal and commercial contexts as well. However, the evidence also suggests that the seven-day week was not yet exclusively used across the empire in the 4th century. Moreover, the habit of dating by the days of the week appeared in only a small percentage of Christian inscriptions and did not become the norm in the 4th century or soon thereafter. Dating by the Kalends, Nones, and Ides remained standard and persisted as such well in the 7th century in the west (Ware 1976).

Conclusion

On the basis of these studies, it would seem that pagans and Christians in the 4th century were much more alike in their notions of the week than Christian preachers were willing to admit. Both pagans and Christians were familiar with and used a seven-day cycle; both were familiar with the astrological associations of each day; both used the planetary names of the days of the week. In these ways, and in the willingness of certain Christian leaders to justify the Christian use of the planetary names of the days of the week, we see a Christian leadership influenced by pagan notions of the week attempting to maintain continuities with their pagan contemporaries.

At the same time, pagans and Christians did have different notions of Sunday; only for the Christians do we have evidence of this day as being marked as a day of worship on a weekly basis, both before and after Constantine. Imperial law, along with Christian preaching, furthered this notion among pagans as well as Christians. But pagan notions of how to celebrate a traditional Roman holiday in honor of Sol, as begun by Constantine, did persist, as indicated by the ongoing celebration of circus games and market days on Sundays. Sunday was still seen by many as the day of the Sun, *dies Solis*—not the day of the Lord, *dies Dominica*—through the end of the 4th century.

Finally, we ought not rely on funerary inscriptions or imperial laws to tell us when the Christian notion of the seven-day week revolving around Sunday as a day of religious observance and rest came to be used exclusively to organize people's time; the seven-day week did not replace other ways of organizing time in the 4th century. Thus, given how gradual was the adoption of celebrating Sunday as a holiday, it seems likely that uniformity in using the seven-day week to regulate people's activities was a post-4th century phenomenon. Only in the 5th century in the West could that be said to be the case, but by then, as the 3rd century author of the *Didascalia* so presciently put it, "all days belong[ed] to the Lord" (6.18.16).

References

Andreau, Jean. "Les Marchés Hebdomadaires du Latium et de Campanie au Ier siècle ap.J.-C." In Elio LoCascio, ed., *Mercati Permanenti e Mercati Periodici nel Mondo Romano*. Bari: Edipuglia, 2000.

Bacchiocchi, Samuele. *From Sabbath to Sunday*. Rome: Pontifical Gregorian University Press, 1977.

Beck, R. "*Qui Mortalitatis Causa Convenerunt:* The Meeting of the Virunum Mithraists on June 26, A.D. 184." *Phoenix* 52 (1998): 335–43.

Beckwith, Roger T., and Wilfred Stott, *This is the Day: the Biblical Doctrine of the Christian Sunday in its Jewish and Early Church Setting*. London: Marshall, Morgan & Scott, 1978.

Böhmer, J. *Der Christliche Sonntag nach Ursprung und Geschichte*. Leipzig, 1931.

Boll, F. "Hebdomas." In *Pauly-Wissowa Real-Encyclopädie der Classischen Altertumswissenschaft* 7, 2. Stuttgart: 1912, 2568–70.

Cameron, Averil, and Stuart G. Hall. *Eusebius, Life of Constantine. Introduction, translation and commentary*. Oxford: Oxford University Press, 1999.

Chastagnol, A. "Le Septième Jour dans *l'Histoire Auguste*." In A. Alföldi, ed., *Antiquitas, Reihe 4, Beiträge zur Historia-Augusta Forschung*. Band 13. Bonn: R. Habelt, 1978, 133–39.

Clauss, Manfred. *The Roman Cult of Mithras*. R. Gordon, trans. New York: Routledge, 2000.

Cotton, Paul. *From Sabbath to Sunday*. Bethlehem, PA: Time Publication Company, 1933.

Degrassi, Attilio. *Inscriptiones Italiae 13: Fasti et elogia, fasc. 2: Fasti Anni Numani et Iuliani*. Rome: 1963.

Dessau, Hermann, ed. *Inscriptiones Latinae Selectae*. Berlin: Weidmann, 1892–1916.

Dekkers, Eligius, and Aemilius Gaar, eds. Hilarius, *Clavis Patrum Latinorum*. Steenbrugis: In Abbatia Sancti Petri, 1961.

Duval, Paul Marie. "Les Dieux de la Semaine." *Gallia* 2 (1953):282–93.

Ferrua, Antonio. "Dal Giorno di Dio al Giorno Degli Dei." *Civiltà Cattolica* 2 (1934):128–43.

Giovanni, Lucio de. *Costantino e il Mondo Pagano*. Naples: University of Naples Press, 1977.

Goldenberg, R. "The Jewish Sabbath in the Roman World up to the Time of Constantine." *Au Aufstieg und Niedergang der romischen Welt* II, 19,1 (1979):442–45.

Grossi Gondi, Felice. *Trattato di Epigrafia Cristiana Latina e Greca del Mondo Romano Occidentale*. Rome: E. Loescher, 1920.

Guarducci, M. "Il graffito Natus Prima Luce nel Mitreo di S. Prisca." *Mysteria Mithrae: Atti del Seminario Internazionale. Roma e Ostia*. Leiden: Brill, 1979.

Handley, Mark A. *Christian Inscriptions of the Late Antique and Early Medieval West: Commemoration and Society in Spain and Gaul, 350–750*. London: University College London Press, 2003.

Hilarius, *De Solstitiis*. B. Botte, ed., *Patrologia Latina Selecta*.

Halsberghe, Gaston H. *The Cult of Sol Invictus*. Leiden: Brill, 1972.

Jory, Edward John, and D. G. Moore, eds. *Corpus Inscriptionum Latinarum* 6. Berlin: 1975.

Kajanto, Iiro. "Dating in the Latin Inscriptions of Medieval and Renaissance Rome." *Arctos* 11 (1977):41–61.

Ligt, L. de. *Fairs and Markets in the Roman Empire*. Amsterdam: Gieben, 1993.

Llewelyn, S. R., and A. M. Nobbs. "The Earliest Dated Reference to Sunday in the Papyri." In S. R. Llewelyn, ed., *New Documents Illustrating Early Christianity 9. A Review of the Greek Inscriptions and Papyri Published in 1986–87*. Grand Rapids, MI: Eerdmans, 2002, 106–18.

Maas, E. *Die Tagesgötter in Rom und den Provincen*. Berlin: 1902.

Meinhold, J. "Sabbat und Sonntag." *Wissenschaft und Bildung 9*. Leipzig: 1909.

Neugebauer, Otto. *The Exact Sciences in Antiquity*. New York: Dover, 1963.

Pietri, Charles. "Le Temps de la Semaine à Rome et dans L'Italie Chrétienne (IV–VIe S.)." In Jean-Marie Leroux, ed., *Le temps Chrétien de la Fin de l'Antiquité au Moyen-Age (III–XIIIe s.), Actes du Colloques Internationales du CNRS No. 604*. Paris: Editions du Centre national de la Recherché Scientifique, 1984, 63–98.

Rordorf, Willy. *Sabbat und Sonntag in der Alten Kirche*. Zurich: Theologischer Verlag, 1972.

———. *Sunday. The History of the Day of Rest and Worship in the Earliest Centuries of the Christian Church*. A. A. K. Graham, trans. [German ed. 1962] London: SCM, 1968.

Salzman, Michele R. *On Roman Time: The Codex-Calendar of 354 and the Rhythms of Urban Life in Late Antiquity*. Berkeley, CA: University of California Press, 1990.

Schürer, E. "Die Siebentagige Woche im Gebrauche der Christlichen Kirche der ersten Jahrhunderte." *Zeitschrift für die Neutestmentliche Wissenschaft und die Kunde des Urchristentums* 6 (1905):1–66.

Shaw, Brent D. "Rural Markets in North Africa." *Antiquités Africaines* 17 (1981):37–84.

Snyder, Walter F. "Quinto Nundinas Pompeis." *Journal of Roman Studies* 26 (1936):12–18.

Stern, Sacha. *Calendar and Community. A History of the Jewish Calendar.* Oxford: Oxford University Press, 2001.

Turcan, Robert. *Mithra et le Mithriacisme.* Paris: Les Belles Lettres, 1993.

Valens, Vettius. *Anthologiarum.* G. Kroll, ed. Berlin: Weidmann, 1908.

Vermaseren, Maarten Jozef. *Corpus Cultus Cybelae Attidisque. III. Italia-Latium.* Leiden: Brill, 1977.

———. *Corpus Inscriptionum et Monumentorum Religionis Mithrae.* Leiden: Hagae Comitis, M. Nijhoff, 1956.

Vermaseren, Maarten Jozef, and C. C. van Essen. *The Excavations in the Mithraeum of the Church of Santa Prisca in Rome.* Leiden: Brill, 1965. M. Beard, J. North, and S. Price, trans. *Religions of Rome.* Cambridge: Cambridge University Press, 1998.

Vidman, Ladislav. *Sylloge Inscriptionum Religionis Isiacae et Sarapiacae.* Berlin: de Gruyter, 1969.

Ware, R. Dean. "Medieval Chronology." In James M. Powell, ed., *Medieval Studies: An Introduction.* Syracuse, NY: Syracuse University Press, 1976, 213–37.

Zerubavel, Eviatar. *The Seven-Day Circle.* New York: Free Press, 1985.

Zöckler, O. "Siebenzahl." In *Pauly-Wissowa Real-Encyclopädie der Classischen Altertumswissenschaft* 18. Stuttgart: J. B. Metzler, 1912, 522.

Contributors

JOHN C. BARRETT, Professor, Department of Archaeology, University of Sheffield.

MARC BRETTLER, Dora Golding Professor of Biblical Studies, Department of Near Eastern and Judaic Studies, Brandeis University.

CHRIS GOSDEN, Lecturer and Curator, Pitt Rivers Museum, Oxford.

ASTRID MÖLLER, Affiliated Scholar, Department of Ancient History, University of Freiburg.

DAVID PANKENIER, Professor of Chinese, Department of Modern Languages and Literature, Lehigh University.

ALEX PURVES, Assistant Professor, Department of Classics, University of California, Los Angeles.

ELEANOR ROBSON, Lecturer, Department of the History and Philosophy of Science, University of Cambridge.

LUDO ROCHER, W. Norman Brown Professor of South Asian Studies Emeritus, Department of Asian and Middle Eastern Studies, University of Pennsylvania.

RALPH M. ROSEN, Professor, Department of Classical Studies, University of Pennsylvania.

MICHELE RENEE SALZMAN, Professor, Department of History, University of California, Riverside.

INDEX

akitu 49, 58, 70, 81, 82
astrolabes 51
al-Biruni 91
Alfred's Castle 4, 36–43
Apollodorus 177, 179
Aristotle 175, 177, 179, 180
Ashur 45, 46, 49, 58–70, 81, 85
Assyria 4, 45–90
astrology 81, 135, 188, 190, 200, 205
astronomical 5, 46, 52, 56, 72, 77, 80, 81, 131
astronomy 5, 48, 77, 79, 80, 82
Augustine 194

Babylonia 4, 45–90
Bali 143
Bible 6, 111–124
bit rimki 73, 81, 82
Book of Changes 7, 133–39, 145
Brahma 94, 95, 103
Bronze Age 3, 12, 18–26, 34–42
Buddhism 96, 97, 98, 99, 101, 105
burial 4, 22, 25, 26, 160, 204, 205

calendar 11, 51–68, 82, 114, 135, 148, 185, 186, 194, 198, 205
celestial motion 72

China 7, 129, 130, 131, 132, 136, 141, 144, 145
Chronicles 120, 172
chronography 8, 9, 170, 173, 175, 177, 180, 182, 183
clay tablets 4, 47
climate 32, 114
Codex Calendar of 354 185, 186, 198, 205
Confucianism 132
Constantine 9, 185–87, 192, 194, 195, 199–202, 206–208
cosmos 89, 100, 106, 132, 135, 137, 147, 155

Dead Sea scrolls 120, 125, 126
Deuteronomistic history 115–27
dharma 93
diastema 171
dies soli 9
divination 80–89, 134–135
Dong Zhongshu 7, 138, 140, 142

Ecclesiastes 6, 112–118, 124–125, 127
eclipse 46, 72, 73, 77, 78, 79
"end of days" 120
Enuma Elish (Epic of Creation) 49, 52

epic of Gilgamesh 48, 69, 80, 81, 85
Esarhaddon 56–59, 61, 63, 66–73, 76, 84
eschatology 120, 121, 123, 125, 127
eschaton 120
eternal return 102, 104, 106
Eusebius 170, 174–184, 200
event and process 13, 15, 19

funerary 26, 189, 202–207

Geertz, C. 138, 143
Genesis 119, 122, 123
Gezer calendar 114

Hellanicus of Lesbos 170
hemerologies 65–68, 80, 81, 87
Hesiod 7, 8, 93, 147–68
Hexagram 7, 139
Hinduism 94–104
Hippias of Elis 8, 173, 176
Homer, *Iliad* 158, 160
Homer, *Odyssey* 158, 162

incantations 63, 76, 77, 80, 81
India 5, 91–110
intercalary year 56
Iphitus, founder of the Olympic Games 176–80
Iron Age 4, 33–43, 149, 150, 151, 152, 154

Jainism 95–101, 110
ji 132, 133, 141

jing 141
Judges, Book of 6, 115–21, 124–26, 199
Jupiter 56, 73, 141
Juvenal 188

kalpa 5, 94–102
kalutu 76, 77, 79, 81, 82
karma 103
kinship 22, 32, 44
Knitting 144
Kronos 155, 159, 162, 164

landscape 26, 32–38, 43, 44
Large ditch systems *see* Linear ditch
Linear ditch 4, 35–36, 38, 42
lunar year 82

Mahàbhàrata 98
Malinowski, J. 143
Manusmriti 95, 98, 101
megalithic tombs 24
mortuary 17, 24, 25
Muses 155, 156

Nabu temple scholars 81
namburbu 68, 76, 80, 81, 82
Neolithic 19, 24, 34
Ninurta 62, 74, 75, 76

Olympic games 8, 169–84
Olympionikon anagraphé 174–80
omen 1, 63, 67, 70, 72, 80, 81, 87
Ouranos 155, 158–64

Paleolithic 19
pancângas 91
Pandora 152, 153, 154, 159, 167
parapegmata 189, 202
pithos 149–53, 159, 167
planetary position 78
portent 46, 68
prediction 48, 55, 77
prophetic literature 120, 121, 122
Purànas 98, 104, 109

Rhea 148, 155, 159
Rigveda 94, 96, 101–104, 107
Roman Britain 42
Romanization 4, 34, 43

seasons 8, 32, 36, 40, 56, 105, 118, 135, 147, 152
Septuagint 115, 120, 122, 126
seven-day week 185–210
solar year 55, 56
Spartan king list 177, 179, 180
spells 63
structural history 12, 14, 19

subsistence and political economies 22
Sumer 63
Sun worship 197
synchronicity 145

Tartaros 162, 163, 164, 165
Tertullian 196, 197, 198, 199
Theodosian Code 185, 199, 201, 202
Titans 158, 162, 163, 164
Trobriand 143, 144
wei 132, 141
West Kennet 24, 25
world ages 5, 91–93, 99–105

yin-yang 131, 134, 135
yuga 5, 93, 95–103, 109

Zerubavel, E. 124, 128, 186, 187, 210
Zeus 8, 152–165
Zielinski, T. 157, 158, 159, 165, 166, 168
zodiac 77, 189
Zuo zhuan 132, 145